"Through fear-busting challenges filled with life-changing truths, *Fear Fighting* will help you identify and overcome the most common fear-triggers of control, people pleasing, worry, comparison, competition, waiting, rejection, opposition, and pain from your past. You will be empowered to live your life with passion, purpose, and an unstoppable, contagious faith!"

**Renee Swope**, author of *A Confident Heart*

"I believe deeply that every person is designed passionately and purposefully by their loving heavenly Father. In her book, Kelly does a beautiful job weaving her own personal story with the transforming truth of God's Word, inviting women to come out of hiding and step into the fullness of their identity as daughters of the King."

**Kyle Zimmerman**, lead pastor, Mariners Church Irvine

"My friend Kelly Balarie has earned a reputation online as an encourager, a fear fighter, and a cheerleader for women across the USA. Now she brings that same voice to the pages of *Fear Fighting*, leading women to a place where they can find the courage to let go of fear and hold tight to Jesus."

**Jennifer Dukes Lee**, author of *The Happiness Dare* and *Love Idol*

"*Fear Fighting* by Kelly Balarie is one of the most thorough and helpful books there is on the subject of fear. Kelly doesn't just say, 'Hey, stop being fearful because God said so!' No, she is in a continual pursuit to battle fear and infuse truth into her own life. And she wants you to do the same. This book is chock-full of practical tips and applications. If you've allowed too much of your life not to be lived because fear has plagued you, this is your book."

**Cindy Beall**, speaker and author of *Rebuilding a Marriage Better Than New*

"*Fear Fighting* is a love letter. It's a love letter from the hand of God to the soul of every world-weary woman who longs to know she's more than her pant size. Kelly Balarie writes with transparency and tenderness, providing practical advice with timely anecdotes. A treasure of a book bound to undo you and bring you home into the heart of the Father."

**Emily T. Wierenga**, founder of The Lulu Tree and author of *Atlas Girl* and *Making It Home*, www.emilywierenga.com

"With beautiful honesty, Kelly Balarie shares important lessons she's learned in her journey from fear to faith. God wants to make fear fighters—and fear vanquishers—of us all!"

**Joanna Weaver**, author of *Having a Mary Heart in a Martha World*

"Kelly Balarie is a prayer warrior, a woman who kno̶w̶'̶ do battle in the places where it matters most, and I k̶n̶ nce that in that place she hears the voice of dear reader, to enter the journey with her rage to be the conqueror you were create

**Logan Wolfram**, sp *covering Hope in the God of Possibility*

"If you're tired of allowing fear to boss and toss you around and you're ready to grow in the peace God has for you, then hang out with Kelly Balarie in the chapters of this book. Through stories and Scriptures, Kelly will challenge and inspire you to take new risks of faith that will lead you to the confidence you long for. A courage that's deeply rooted in the strength of Jesus."

**Gwen Smith**, author of *I Want It All* and *Broken into Beautiful* and cofounder of Girlfriends in God

"In *Fear Fighting*, Kelly Balarie teaches us to identify, call out, and overcome the fear inducers of life. With vulnerability and grace, Kelly leads us to the only overcoming power available to humankind, trust in Jesus Christ alone. If you have ever struggled with the kind of fear that seeks to derail, demolish, or destroy you or those you love, this book will awaken you to know and walk in divine courage."

**Jan Greenwood**, pastor of Pink, Gateway Women and author of *Women at War*

"In her book *Fear Fighting*, Kelly pinpoints an intriguing aspect of our culture today. Many are trapped in fear and brokenness, but not without hope. Kelly presents a beautiful guide, steeped in God's Word, on how to break free and move forward in faith toward God's perfect plan for your life."

**Micca Campbell**, national speaker and author of *An Untroubled Heart*

"In spite of everything—our failures, our fears, our worries, our attempted control of our own lives—God loves us. He adores us. And if you don't believe me, read Kelly Balarie's *Fear Fighting*. She has lived with fear, faced countless challenges, and learned that God is the answer to it all. I think every single one of us can benefit from her encouraging insights and practical tips. There's something in here for you. I'm sure of it!"

**Kelly O'Dell Stanley**, author of *Praying Upside Down* and *Designed to Pray*

"Kelly Balarie speaks with conviction, compassion, and a keen understanding of what prevents our best life possible with God. If you've ever struggled with fear—who hasn't?—and you need a motivating nudge in the right direction, this book is for you. Whether your biggest obstacles are mental or physical, *Fear Fighting* can help you persevere and faithfully confront your challenges by relying on the unlimited strength of the Holy Spirit and the ultimate power of God."

**Kari Kampakis**, blogger and author of *Liked: Whose Approval Are You Living For?* and *10 Ultimate Truths Girls Should Know*

"Blending Scripture, prayers, stories, and a poetic voice, Kelly reminds us how beloved we are of God and how God uses us mightily in the places we see as weaknesses. With creativity and passion, Kelly takes us on journeys of hope and redemption so we can be free to live into all that God has for each of us."

**Dr. Heather Wright**, executive director of Greenwich Center for Hope and Renewal, licensed professional counselor, author of *Redeeming Eve* and *Small Group Leadership as Spiritual Direction*, and coauthor of *Sacred Stress: A Radically Different Approach to Using Life's Challenges for Positive Change*

"Put on your boxing gloves and get ready to punch fear in the face. Filled with biblical truth, Balarie's words remind us that God's great love empowers us to live life to the fullest and leave fear in the dust."

**Jill Lynn Buteyn**, coauthor of *Just Show Up*

"Armed with the truth of God's Word, Kelly Balarie's book is one that should be savored chapter by chapter. With the study guide, it is especially valuable to women's Bible studies, community groups, and local gatherings. The content, depth, and personal relevance make the vague idea of fear fighting applicable."

**Sue Stuart**, teaching director of Community Bible Study,
Westport, Connecticut

"Kelly gets real about the negative impact of fear and worry. She offers a process and support for those in the fear-fighting battle to help them find hope and peace. An excellent read!"

**Courtney DeFeo**, author of *In This House, We Will Giggle*
and founder of Lil Light O' Mine

"Fuel your spirit through the fearless and tangible encouragement of Kelly Balarie as she leads you on a journey to demolish fear. This book will inspire you to stop hiding behind your excuses and step into the treasure of God's calling on your life. You will soon find you are not alone. With God on your side and a new community of fear-fighting friends, nothing is impossible!"

**Angela Craig**, director of the NWMN Women in Ministry
and author of *Pivot Leadership: Small Steps . . . Big Change*

"Kelly encourages us to risk being vulnerable with ourselves, with God, and with others in order to let the Lord step in, heal our past, and awaken us in courage to fight the stronghold of fear. She challenges us to bond together in love and move forward boldly together to make an impact for the Lord and be the change-makers He designed us to be. This book is an inspiration every person needs to read!"

**Nikki Carlson**, cofounder of ChicBuds and ChicExecs

"Kelly is a champion for women, and with this book she will take your hand and walk with you into battle—against fear, against anxiety, against the enemy. If you struggle to be as brave as you want to be and as free as you were made to be, *Fear Fighting* is the tool you need."

**Mary Carver**, coauthor of *Choose Joy: Finding Hope
and Purpose When Life Hurts*

"Kelly's voice is so familiar that you will feel like you are sitting down with a best friend as you read this book. The best part is that you will feel like this friend is for you: that she understands whatever you might tell her, that she has been there too, and that she wants to go to battle with you."

**Kathryn Maack**, fellowship women's pastor, Fellowship Bible Church,
Little Rock, Arkansas

"*Fear Fighting* is an honest and brave gift to readers. Kelly's heart for women to be set free from fears' limitations bleeds through every page. This book is for anyone desiring an action plan to kick fear to the curb."

**Lisa Bishop**, director of women's leadership development
and women's ministry, Park Community Church

"In her book *Fear Fighting*, author and self-confessed fearer Kelly Balarie grabs us by the heart and invites us to journey to places of truth where God delights to stir hope. With unmistakable authenticity, she exposes the soul cracks of our cluttered, broken lives shaken with fear, shame, and hiding and flings open windows of faith toward a view of a Spirit-led life of boldness."

**Jan Kern**, author, speaker, life coach, and founder of Voice of Courage,
www.voiceofcourage.org

"*Fear Fighting* is a message from God's own heart. It exposes the lies we've been believing for way too long and reminds us that the truth is better than we could have ever imagined. Be prepared to find new hope and strength as you become a fear fighter too!"

**Susan Pettrey**, women's ministry director, The Brooklyn Tabernacle

"As Kelly Balarie takes you on her journey of fighting fears using proclamations, Scripture, and practical daily helps, you'll realize after the first riveting chapter that it's becoming your own personal journey. A journey that will bring new life to dead places and victory instead of defeat. A must-read for any woman who is honest enough to admit that fighting fear requires a power greater than herself and intentional application of truth!"

**Debbie Hopper**, director of women's ministry, Seacoast Church,
Mt. Pleasant, South Carolina

"Kelly's laughter-infused conversation pulls back the cloak of fear to reveal the schemes of the enemy who seeks to destroy us and the One who will equip us, walk with us, stand with us, and hold us while we cry—Jesus. If you need a shot of courage to fight back against the enemy, you will find it here in Kelly's book."

**Shanelle Wagner**, minister to women, First Denton Church, Denton, Texas

"In two words, this book is nothing less than *fresh revelation* from heaven. *Fear Fighting* is a wonderful and powerful addition to the libraries of people looking for heavenly ammunition against what is often our most sinister earthly enemy."

**Marlinda Ireland, DMin**, writer, speaker, and cofounder of Christ Church

"Kelly has the gift of speaking Holy Spirit–saturated words into fear spaces. Her passion and honesty carry a courageous momentum as though you are reading spoken word. You can't help but be swept up in the sheer bravery of her voice. Upon turning the final page of *Fear Fighting*, you will experience a newfound purpose, peace, and confidence in your created self."

**Bekah Jane Pogue**, speaker and author of *Choosing Real*

# FEAR
# *Fighting*

awakening
courage to
OVERCOME
your fears

## KELLY BALARIE

BakerBooks

*a division of Baker Publishing Group*
Grand Rapids, Michigan

Published by Baker Books
a division of Baker Publishing Group
P.O. Box 6287, Grand Rapids, MI 49516-6287
www.bakerbooks.com

Printed in the United States of America

Library of Congress Cataloging-in-Publication Data
Names: Balarie, Kelly, 1978– author.
Title: Fear fighting : awakening courage to overcome your fears / Kelly Balarie.
Description: Grand Rapids : Baker Books, 2017. | Includes bibliographical references.
Identifiers: LCCN 2016031069 | ISBN 9780801019340 (pbk.)
Subjects: LCSH: Christian women—Religious life. | Fear—Religious aspects—Christianity.
Classification: LCC BV4527 .B345 2017 | DDC 248.8/43—dc23
LC record available at https://lccn.loc.gov/2016031069

The author is represented by MacGregor Literary, Inc.

17  18  19  20  21  22  23        7  6  5  4  3  2

To Emanuel: you are my coauthor. You are my coach. You are my fan. But most of all you are the one who pushed me not to fear my dream and not to run from it, but instead—to grab it. No words would be on this page without you, that I know. My gratefulness and admiration for all things *you* runneth over. You bless me, undeservedly, again and again. I hope God pays you back for that.

# Contents

Contents

# Introduction

## *Fear Fighters Unite*

Avoiding danger is no safer in the long run than outright exposure. The fearful are caught as often as the bold.

Helen Keller

*I* still fear. I do. If you were hoping for a perfect, brave, bold, amazing, and beautifully clad woman wearing the badged heart of courage, I am not your gal. I am gaining ground but I have miles to go. I have pushed through some swamplands but I still have a whole world to traverse. I have been touched deeply by the Spirit but I fight daily to stay above ground. My heart is unsettled because only sometimes I feel not anxious, only sometimes I feel okay, and only sometimes I wholeheartedly believe God—and sometimes is just not enough. It isn't. There's no such thing as partial faith. You know it and I know it. And saying this? Ouch! It hurts.

I am tired. I am tired of pretending I am good. I am tired of just existing. I am tired of returning to swampy places that make me sink into selfish desires. Instead, I am ready to tread somewhere different, somewhere brave, and somewhere new—or at least I think I am.

I dream of this verdant place. I daydream about it. I wish for it. And, when I finally get kind of serious about it, I pray for it. Are you at all like me? My hands are open and this book is my beacon of hope, my steadfast calling to go all the way—to let my heart fly, completely free, into the glorious sky where I risk it all to go the full distance, just God and me. Two who can do anything and go anywhere when they pull together. With this, I'm pretty confident (as confident as a fearful girl can get) I'll look back one day and say, "It was a dangerous, dark, and unsteady world, but the Spirit and me, we made it, we survived. Thank God I tried, because in this crazy adventure of amazingness, I couldn't have done it without Him."

I like this idea, because then, on my final day, I won't look back fretting that I forgot God and feeling like I lived a half-baked life. I won't. Instead, I'll know death isn't the end and life is just the beginning. In that moment, rather than agonizing over myself, I'll delight in His magnificent return because, in my life, I chose to know Him intimately, passionately, and reliantly. I'll look back and remember how I rested my rapid-beating heart right up against Him often. I'll remember His love that held me. It will be a victory day. I'll pump my arms and confidently walk right up into God's open embrace, and we will move on to something better. I look forward to that.

### Joining Hands

So I reach my hand out to you. To one who probably, like me, either feels removed from the good things of life or alive to the continually recycling factory of worry. Either way, will you do this thing with me? Because maybe, just maybe, if we join hands and take a small step—rather than look to judge each other's nail polish—we can actually make some progress. Maybe if we link arms rather than put our arms up in defense, we'll actually find ourselves united in boldness rather than divided and living in unhappiness. Maybe if we pull together rather than pulling out our worries of what "they" think—or what is about to ruin us—we'll make headway. Maybe we will arrive somewhere good.

Call me crazy, but I believe it's possible and I really want to get somewhere, don't you? Somewhere new, somewhere just a little bit risky, somewhere a little more free, somewhere lighter. Somewhere *more*. I see it on the horizon. Calling.

And staying where we are stinks worse than a giant landfill. Why stay here? Why stay in the place where we brace ourselves for the next thing about to nail us? Where we determine rejections are eternal verdicts on our worth. Where we swing on the pendulum of comparison—prideful one day and ruined the next. Where we are jealous of anyone who is better. Where our past stunts our growth. Where we shake horribly at the idea of the unknown. These kinds of things wear a good girl down to the treads.

They've worn me down and they keep wearing me down. They've kept me from friends and fun and fantastic opportunities. They've made me timid and shy, overly aggressive and nagging, mean and terse. They've been little dictators that have walked away with my dreams, my future, and my hope. I want to fight back now. I see how they rob. I see how much I could have had. I see how those around me have suffered because of my actions.

I want to start fighting today. Because I want devotion. I want rhythm with God. I want to do life with Him.

Friends, the Spirit's work in me through this book—it is my only hope. I want to see what happens when one girl lays it all down as if everything depends on it and goes all-in to chase bravery with God.

Is it a risk? Yes. What if the Spirit doesn't show up? My disbelief says that's possible, but I'd rather discover truth than live a lie.

To dive into this little experiment, friends, I need you. I need accountability, support, and a hand to make it all the way. Just knowing that we are a united band of women means that we can be authentic and transparent in this neck of these scary ol' woods. It is imperative we stand united so when fear tries to knock us over into failure (which tends to disguise itself as the pursuit of perfection), we rise as a red-rover band of women unbroken.

When you get silent and introspective, what patterns of fear do you identify in your life? I don't know about you, but I see how these patterns wreck me. They keep me hurt in false comfort. They keep me crying in fake safety. They keep me shivering in isolation. We live these patterns without thinking twice, don't we? On autopilot, we figure things will somehow work out and we will land at our predetermined destination—until one day we wake up and see that the distance between who we are and who we want to be is the width of the United States. Then we hate ourselves.

Truth is, normal doesn't deliver, status quo doesn't work, and pilots find themselves lost if they fall asleep. We won't sleep; we will rise up to allow the mystery of the Spirit to remove normal and bring in paranormal renewal. Not in some extraterrestrial way, but in a way that blows our mind because we never really believed it was possible.

## Mobilizing Our Fear Fight

It will be a battle. It won't be easy, that I know. But nothing's ever easy that is worth anything. There is no treasure without a seeker. There is hardly gold without a hunt. There is no diamond without pursuit. We will do all of these things. We will chase God and we will find Him. We will dig through our beliefs, wipe away the grime of lies, and discover our sparkle once again. We will adventure—and find the Spirit's affection and liberation for poor fearful souls like ours. It won't just be our fight; it will also be God's—on our behalf.

In high heels, we will fight. In skirts, we will fight. In pearls, we will fight. In the midst of the mayhem of work, womanhood, kids, or husbands, we will fight. Not like some image of perfection, but like women who aren't afraid to let their mascara run in zebra stripes as they run in hot pursuit of real-life change. This means the tears will fall, my fellow fearers, but our arms won't, for we will also knock down any force that tries to block us. Arms crossed, breathing stable, we will learn to say, "Enough. If I can't be me, I can't be free."

We will not go alone. The Spirit will be our coach; His emboldened fighters never lose. They don't lose because they realize they are loved. They don't hear lies because they know how to discern the whisper of truth. They don't live injured and insecure because they see the indwelling power of what Christ has entrusted within them. They don't add lighter fluid to shame because the Spirit knits security in them. They don't live in agony because they live in awe of what God is doing in the present, in the here and the now.

We will dig out this treasure by the influence of the Spirit—in a profound way. In a way where we are confident it is ours for the hunting, finding, and owning. Then we will turn around to grab this bucking and unruly thing called the unknown (see Heb. 11:1), and we will put it to rest by faith instead of warring it down with fear. We will go one way instead of the other, more and more—not perfectly but purposely—and we will learn to discern the still, small voice of God (see 1 Kings 19:12). A voice that speaks calm.

Lean in. Breathe in. Relax.

Let go of pressures. The fight is nothing more than willingness and readiness. And I can't wait to do this with you; it is sure to be a journey of excitement, revelation, wisdom, and discovery. It will be a journey of growth, of veracity and new birth. Best of all, it will be an adventure we will trek together.

We will break the pressure that sits on our backs so we don't break under life's circumstances. *We will surface.*

We will shatter all antiGod images and fight the labels we bow down to so that we can light God's real truth in us. *We will shine.*

We will meditate on truth and uncover the deep knowledge found only in God's Word. *We will learn.*

We will meet other women who have struggled through their own fear fits. *We will join hands.*

*We will learn to live like beloved daughters who know their Daddy.*

And together *we will speak boldness*—new, despair-halting decrees, such as:

*Fear, you are a bad friend. But I serve a great God.*

*Fear, you are enemy number-one. But Christ has already won.*

*Fear, you are against me. But God is for me.*

My pledge to you? I will only be the truest form of myself. I realize if we want to get through this—through debilitating things like dealing with problem people, panic-packed predicaments, and painful pasts—it's the only way to go.

I want to see it work for me. I am going all-in with you.

Right into the nearly unreachable depths of this love, where the Spirit spins a woman called a fear fighter.

A fear fighter doesn't look around but rather inside for strength. She doesn't back down to naysayers but says God will help her. She doesn't see the waves as waters ready to sink her but floats to new heights.

She doesn't fear the truth but voices it, knowing it heals. She doesn't live a fake faith but finds a small seed within and nurtures it. She doesn't feel like a puppet, moving to the sway of the world, but dances.

She loses herself in vast Love to find herself loved. She will be you and she will be me, only by the power of the Holy Spirit.

Let's go.

# Part 1

## Coming to God
# Jumpy, Jittery,
### and Just
# Needing Help

## *one*

# Discovering
# the Power of Now

I think that sometimes being fearless is having fears but jumping anyway.

Taylor Swift

*Get out of my way! I am on a mission*. I didn't say it aloud, but I might as well have. I was on a mission! A critical one that seemed almost impossible, as I could see a long line of people ahead of me inside the coffee shop. These people should know to never get between a woman and her morning caffeine fix. That's how I figured it. It would be just the thing to send all the dominos of my day falling.

I couldn't have that.

With all the details of my skinny, extra hot, double pump vanilla latte on my mind, I nearly missed him. My feet carried me faster than a cartoon roadrunner—and let's be honest, there's no time for anything when you have the anxiety of time chasing your heels. *Must. Get. Coffee. Have. No. Time.*

But there he sat. Scrunched in the corner by the door. Humble. Lowly. Dirty. One you would certainly miss if you weren't looking. But I didn't miss him; he was staring intently. His eyes met mine with both invitation and conviction. They practically asked me, *Are you just like them? Another one rushing past me to get that cup of golden idol to warm your hands for the day?*

Everything in me wanted to snap back, "Well, yes, I am. And don't talk to me anymore, because I am going to be stuck at the back of that line. And then you'll have to deal with one angry lady and no money in your cup, sir, and you certainly don't want that."

I almost said it. I really wanted to. I wanted to ignore him and rush in to suck down that brown nectar from the green goddess. But I didn't. I didn't because sometimes you know it is the voice of God pulling you in to something great, and if you don't slow down and listen for just a minute, you'll miss it.

I stopped. I stopped because I was deathly afraid of missing something greater, something powerful, or something that would release the feeling that an unbound schedule meant I would plummet straight into dark depths of despair. So I took the risk. I drew near, and the closer I got the more I couldn't help but inhale his stench and observe his deep, dirty lines of life-pain. I didn't want all this heaviness on my rush-in and rush-out stop-off. I knew this daily twenty-one-minute commute inside-out, and pausing now would throw my whole day off.

Yet what I have realized is that stopping and stepping into unsafe forces us to receive God's new safe. Will we risk it? Will we receive it?

It's the only place we get to see that God won't turn His back on us, disregard our emotions, or critique us. Rather He'll speak straight into our gaps of discomfort—if we let Him.

Will we?

I wish I could tell you, as that man and I talked, that I was given some glory story with words so powerful they made my insides settle like peaceful, early morning fog, but I can't. Our shared words are mostly blurred in my memory now, but the underlying message of this encounter can't be erased: shushing up and slowing down is paramount to God working in us—and strengthening us. The truth is, God is ready to hit us with unfathomable new perspectives—ones that redefine our past, present, and problems if we will only stop, receive, and consider.

Will we? Will we walk unafraid into His presence? Into God's rhythms? Not cowering from mysteries?

You see—that man and I? We both had needs that day, though maybe we didn't even know what we needed. Maybe we didn't know why we reached out to each other. Maybe our lack of knowledge didn't matter. God knew. He positioned that man at the door and me heading to it. He set up a blind date founded on the principle of love—and waited for the celebration to unfold. God's deep affection was stored up in this chance connection of two unlikely souls. It often is, if only we stop, receive, and consider.

What if I had pretended like I couldn't see or hear him and just kept walking?

It pains me to think how I could have missed his eyes. Eyes that looked into mine the same way mine looked into his. Eyes that understood. Eyes that said, *I see you. I care for you. It is hard out there.* Even more, it pains me to think there was a chance I could have missed God's great collision that wanted to break up my don't-get-too-close-to-me mentality. Oh, I thank God I didn't miss out. I thank God I didn't miss His small prompting of, *I see what you are going through. I know you.*

I stopped. Received. Considered.

God knew both what he needed and what I needed.

This show called life—although we think it's about us, it hardly is at all. There is so much more to it. When we open our eyes to the greater possibilities, we enter an immersive experience where love comes alive, where the pin-drop nature of God's whispers are heard, and where the form of who we were actually made to be emerges. We hardly need scripts, because the whole point of unconditional love is that it's entirely unscripted. We don't have to know everything but just have to be willing to accept His everything. To let it settle right into the deep gashes of fear. Then, things change.

## Don't Miss It!

Now I can't help but think that some of you might look at this story and say, "So what? You slowed down? You met a man who celebrated God with you, and that's nice. But what does this have to do with me?"

A whole lot. If you spend your whole life grasping for happy in the future, you'll end up missing God's transformation in the present. You'll run after something but you'll never catch it. I know this to be true because I have lived this way. And one thing I have come to terms with is that if we want the Spirit's power to crush our momentary fear, the only place that will happen is in the here and now.

Will we believe God can change us right here, or will we continue to pull on a wishbone and hope our best dreams come true?

I know, my collaborators in fear, that many of you are just like me. And in this moment, right here, your excitement is starting to wither. Why? Because you've hardly lived in the moment and you feel horrible about that. Let me tell you something: God does not point His finger at you. He doesn't give you demerits. He doesn't send you to your room without dinner. He speaks life. Let's allow it to soak into us and be with Him in this very moment:

*Child, I am with you. I will strengthen and help you; I will uphold you (Isa. 41:10). You can feel afraid, but know this: I will sustain you no matter what—I will not let you fall (Ps. 55:22). Still feel anxious? Pray. Petition. Offer thanksgiving. And let My peace waterfall on you (Phil. 4:6–7). I give you My peace; don't you believe?*

*It is peace I leave and peace I give, not like this mad world offers but as only I can—so don't even fuss with all that madness (John 14:27). Turn your shortness of breath into deep breaths, for you have not been given a spirit of fear but of power and love and a sound mind (2 Tim. 1:7). You don't have to fear the intensity of love; you see, My perfect love casts out fear (1 John 4:18). My consolation is what will bring joy (Ps. 94:19). Come, get to know Me. Come, get to see how much I care about your crossed arms, your shaking hands, your jitters, and your all-over-cold sweats. I see it all, and guess what, My child: there is no condemnation for those who are in Christ Jesus (Rom. 8:1). So pull up a chair and let Me do what I do best: minister to your heart murmurs.*

I don't want to let these words fly by unnoticed. I don't want to stay the same. Do you?

Part of beating what you always do is realizing what it is. I know that I am prone to stay in the status quo, like a teenager with her head stuck in her smartphone, both avoiding and dissing instruction.

Just thinking of this also makes me think of my son. Sometimes I have to tell him to put on his listening ears. Normally this happens when I am on the verge of going berserk, and after I have repeated myself for the fourth, fifth, or sixth time—and my insides are about to spill rage all over the kitchen floor. It is my last-ditch effort that says, *This is the moment when you absolutely must listen.* It is the moment when everything is on the line if he doesn't hear me. It is both my way to ensure things don't fly over his head and to really reach deep into his heart.

With this in mind, I wonder: Will we put on our listening ears to hear God?

*Father God, we don't want to miss You anymore. Will You help us to hear the call to be brave? We believe, by faith, in Your power to teach us, to lead us, and to help us venture to the heights we are deathly afraid of. Illuminate these paths by the current of Your Spirit. But most of all, give us eyes to see and ears to hear through the entirety of this book. Amen.*

## No One Said It's Easy

When I look at myself, I see a girl who wants to be brave but isn't so certain she actually can be. I love all those generic affirmation memes online—*Go, woman, go!* and *Nothing can stop you!* and *You are better than yourself.* Half of me gravitates to them, wishing they were true, but after reading a hundred and one of them, I have never seen them work a single thing in my life and I never really even feel that well just five minutes after reading one. I call them half-baked solutions to a crippling problem.

I am left discouraged; after all, I have tried it all. I have tried to will myself into better thinking: *Kelly, you can do it, stop fearing.* I have tried to chide myself into better thinking: *Kelly, you will never pull yourself together if you act like this.* I have even tried to shame myself into confidence: *Kelly, you are going to push everyone away with your bad anxiety.*

When all these efforts fail, I normally give up and give in to some sort of pleasure to get my mind off it: TV, food, drink, movie—you name it, I know it.

Even talking about this induces my other cure-all answer that is easy to offer: *Kelly, give 'em Jesus. He will make everything all right.*

But things didn't look "all right" for Jesus. Things weren't all peaches and sugar with a dollop of whipped cream on top. They were hard. They were painful. They were tough.

Jesus never said to expect easy. So why do we?

And maybe this is the exact kind of encouragement I really need. I need to know someone gets me. Someone understands. Someone declares it hard. Someone has been down a road with a debilitating cross on His back as He pushed into real life. Knowing this, I won't feel so alone and scared. Then I can maybe see how He made it—and not just made it but made it safely *home*—and how He makes sense out of everything, even the little things, the pains and threats of today.

It is not so much that I don't have to be struggling as it is just that I have to get after Jesus and bring Him into my struggle with me. Doing this—it is called *chasing brave*.

## Open Your Eyes to the Landscape of Now

When I really stop to think about it, I can't help but notice yesterday is gone, done, finished, and complete. Tomorrow, also, encapsulates everything a fearer fears. But today holds a new horizon of opportunity. It is like a blank canvas, available to portray any image that God deems right for it. I can enter today ready to be changed. Willing to dance in the wind or care for a lost soul or be a child again or speak up for the marginalized. I can move.

The Spirit paints new life in us as we open ourselves up to His movement.

Are you His blank canvas?

*Now* is the only ground where transformation can be found. It is the only place where a new image of you and me can surface and breathe and live.

This untamed and unconstrained movement splashes vivid colors both left and right. It brings new growth from old seeds. It brings vibrancy to dullness. And it ends up sounding an awful lot like this:

*Now I am going to change you.*
*Now I am going to do something new.*
*Now My Spirit will lead you.*
*Now My Spirit will counsel you.*
*Now My eye will show you the way to go, and you will.*

*Now I will come to your rescue.*

*Now you will find My hand, and I will not let you fall.*

*Now I want you to trust Me.*

*Now I have somewhere to take you.*

*Now see yourself as Mine.*

*Now know you are My daughter.*

*Now journey with Me.*

*Now spin.*

*Now be free.*

*Now come undone.*

*Now let go.*

Our heart beats. Our breath resumes. Our hands relax. Our motions settle. Our will lays down. Our dreams surface. Our being is being in Him. Our eyes want to see His will. And what happens, what we unearth, is *her*. That little girl. The one who once just enjoyed the beach as the beach and wasn't distracted by all the hazards and car messiness and screamers that come along with it.

We pull her out, we remove her shell, and all is revealed—we see all we don't need and so much of what is, in us. We see all we hope to be and a willingness to grab much more. And so we relax and we let go. We are that little girl again.

We dance with the thrill of creativity. Arms wide open, we swirl with no agenda. We permit the peace of wind to lightly toss our hair. We find our motion and move to the beat of carelessness.

Free-spiritedness unhinges us with every salt-laced breath we take. Sand runs through our fingers. The sun closes the moment as it reaches the horizon and the sky offers us a colorful gift.

We find presence. The Spirit moves and then we do—according to truth. We move simply, in the here and now.

Don't miss it. *Here* is where God is.

Sure, we can plan tomorrow, sit in old grudges, pulse with anxiety over sunburns, or break down with the fear that our kids will get a cold and then we'll get a cold. We can do that—but then we may as well say, "Adios, joy; hello, turbulence!"

I am tired of that old cycle, aren't you? I no longer want to be so consumed with chasing wild notions that I miss the Spirit's motion.

The wind reminds us that He is always with us (and always will be). *Presence.*

The air proves He is around us. *Safety.*

The light reflects on us. *Power.*

The sand is vast around us. *Love.*

The water runs in rhythms that don't end. *Faithfulness.*

Peace fills our moment. *Life.*

A glimpse of heaven is close enough to grasp. *Vision.*

We speak new despair-halting decrees that help us chase brave. We say:

*If the Spirit is working here, then here is where I must be.*

*God's working ground is the training ground of boldness.*

*Joy isn't recovered from the past; it is only celebrated in the present.*

We start thinking differently and then we start living differently, until some fine day we look down and see we are actually getting well. We see an image on a canvas of us chasing brave, and we feel good. We may even fly. All things are possible; we don't need to know. Either way, we love the feeling and we say, "It's a miracle. Thank You, God."

## Something to Chew On

**The Art of Hearing God:** Wake in the morning and let the Word of God tend to your heart. Search out verses on fear, hope, courage, and life, and write them as a love letter from God to yourself. Then go deeper. Ask God to reveal an area in your life where you need to hold on to a specific verse or point. Listen.

**Panic, Blood Pressure, and Stress-Reducing Prayer**

*Spirit God, pull me from my slumber. Shock the eyes of my heart. Light a spark within me. Pull me close to You. Call out to me when I cannot hear. Flood discouragement with Your presence. Indulge me in Your love. Shine the light of hope so I can find the shore beyond the wrecking and warring waters. For then I will walk on the safety that lets the past be past and the future materialize as bearable. Confirm my steps, grow me in boldness, armor me in strength, and recommission me in love. Amen.*

# two
# Dodging Obstacles

Fire is the test of gold; adversity, of strong men.

Seneca the Younger

*A*re you at all like me? Do you wake up and instantly begin making quick calculations of all that could go wrong, and then try to figure out how you will survive? Most days I am convinced there is a whole lot of junk coming at me. I am convinced that by 8:00 I will be running late, by 11:00 I will be stuck in traffic, by 2:00 I will be in tears, and then I'll head straight into a pile of work that is impossible to accomplish. At day's end? Kids will throw fits and mountains of dishes are sure to await.

No wonder I feel anxious.

I haven't always lived this terrorized by life, I really haven't—or so I would like to tell you—but I think some stuff in life got me messed up along the way. This reality sometimes makes me ask myself, *How do you chase God when a whole lot of cruddy stuff is always nipping at your heels?*

## Where's Super-Slick Shiny God?

I remember when I was about to become a newlywed. New husband-to-be. New house-to-come. New Jesus. It was a shiny time. It was a fun time. It's the type of time you want to take a picture of, frame, and leave untouchable. You do this because, as all fearers know, eventually the hammer does come down and your worst dream comes true—and everything will shatter in the blink of an eye. You can't let things break; that's always the goal. Keep things together.

I didn't succeed. My husband's brother died in an unexpected accident right before our wedding. My husband's company went tumbling under right before our wedding. My family expressed uncertainty about our marriage right before our wedding. Doubts emerged right before our wedding. We stood looking at a pile of debt stacked up to the amount of $40,000 right before our wedding.

A dark cloud settled over us.

It blocked the light of God. I did some desperate things. I got doubt-filled and discouraged. I sank under the waves rather than letting God's hand hold me above them. I recycled worries again and again, all the while hating myself for doing it.

Ever been there?

Light leaves and darkness arrives, and with all that's happening, you're pretty sure you're going to be left cold and shivering. It is as if, in this moment, you're convinced God finally ran out of patience with your bad attitude and is now dropping you off on the side of the road. "Get out—and find your own way home!"

"God! Don't leave!" we say.

But we figure it is already a done deal.

God deserted us, so we desert God. "Fine. We don't need you anyway," we say, "We'll make our own way."

As I stared at my supposed-to-be-perfect newlywed home, the room spun with all the burdens sitting on my shoulders. *I can't pay that bill, which means I can't pay all the others. If I don't pay those, the credit companies will come after me, which means I will never be able to buy a home, which means my kids will be sad when we sell their toys and when we downgrade houses. Of course, they will hate their mom, which means I will be a nightmare of a wife, which means I will be hated by everyone—which means you, God, are leaving me deserted and left for ruin. Thanks a lot!*

I went to play basketball, figuring some exercise would help me let off some steam. But the ball crashed down and cracked my finger nearly in two, and then things went from bad to worse. The experts said I would need costly surgery. I didn't know how I was going to make it through. Bam! Tears! Fears! More frustration!

God was long gone and I was going downhill fast. Of course, I wouldn't have told you this. I would have nodded my head and said, "Yes, God is good. God will provide. God loves me." But my insides would have told a different story. My insides would have seen that shiny picture crumbling a bit more and convulsed with my powerlessness to do anything about it.

I had no idea how the money was going to surface, if God would actually return to pick me up again, or if I would have to resort to hitchhiking or some other deplorable act to find my way home.

*Where did God go? When I became a Christian I thought I signed up for shiny!*

## Go Ahead, Take off Your Shoes and Get Holy

At this point in my life, it was a daily task to figure out how to keep breathing. But, like I said before, when you're chasing God and you finally shut up, the Spirit has a way of holding you in your time of need. I suppose this is why He's called Counselor (John 14:26); He brings to mind those life-restoring Words of God that counsel you. I like that. I need counseling.

His Word to me at that time sounded like this: "Take off your sandals, for the place where you are standing is holy ground" (Exod. 3:5).

*Ahem. Now, God? Here? At work? The stench will kill 'em! What in the world does that mean—remove my shoes?*

But let me tell you something, and I am serious about this: when you stop thinking God's Words in the Bible are crazy and don't apply to you, you suddenly realize—they do. You feel life open up to plains you never realized existed. You just have to drive over the hump of uncertainty and keep going. It doesn't happen overnight but rather with a fight, and that is what we are doing here.

Then things happen. You hold a broken picture but see it differently—a new image appears. You say unheard of and practically ludicrous things. Things like, "Well, God, I have nothing to add. You hold everything, so let's go—and do it Your way." It's almost like God lent you His glasses.

You get clarity. Focus, even.

Lights flick on and the Spirit delivers a tailored message arrowed straight to your heart (Eph. 5:8). All you know is you got pinged by *sense*. Sense that pushes you toward what you were always meant to do and created to be.

Certainly you know it can't be your doing, because it was far easier than any harebrained scheme you could ever concoct. You couldn't just drive yourself up to a launching pad called hope and take off.

I recently read about a woman with tetrachromatic vision. For those lucky few with this genetic mutation, the world appears like a kaleidoscope of vibrancy. While we see leaves as shades of green, they may see them in shades of pinks, purples, blues, and greens kicked up to the nth degree. Everything is highlighted, eye-catching, and vivid. In fact, tetrachromats see one hundred times more color than the average human. The more they train their eye to look, the more they can behold. Life is a living painting and they are smack dab in the center of it; they can literally touch and feel surrounding brilliance, like HD on steroids. I envy their view; their world is more than meets the eye.[1]

What if we had the chance to see from a more vibrant perspective? It gets me thinking that, with the Spirit, we are kind of tetrachromatic. Suddenly we get eyes to see and ears to hear with vividness that we never understood before (Matt. 13:16). The spectrum of possibility opens up, variances of new hope set in, and filters of truth hit the tones of our life just right. We step back for a moment and suddenly we see things don't look so much broken as they are a work in progress.

*Aha* moments become abundant.

The Spirit is a luminous perspective-changer. He takes the dulls and sharpens them bright in such a way that we can't help but step closer, grab hold of our once-hated barrier, and say, "Wow. Look at you. I never thought I could see you that way. Aren't you something to consider?"

That is what He did with me. The Spirit illuminated a grain of something I needed. So you know what I did? I looked left and right, and then I did it; I took off my shoes—odor and all.

I chose to believe my sinking (or stinky) ground was holy ground. I took off my shoes. Taking off your shoes means:

Listening to God above humankind's diatribe.

Seeing God's bigger picture, not a shattered one.

Getting reverent instead of existent in pain.

Being open to truth instead of closed up in lies.

Trusting refinement versus never-ending ailments.

Seeing God's plan above your immediate goals.

Letting God see your grime so He can wash it clean.

Yelling, screaming, and pleading to be heard and helped.

It doesn't always look pretty, but it is almost always effective. I gave it a shot. I got myself settled into the idea of getting holy before God. The Spirit even called out on my behalf, I am sure of it. He does that, you know? He speaks our unspeakable needs (Rom. 8:26). He groans our groans and cares for our cares. And something transcendent happened. I felt heaviness leave, burdens flee, and a new fire take form. If it was on film it would have been an IMAX experience, I am sure, because my nearsighted eyes felt intricate depths of unparalleled understanding.

It's not like I could say, "Grab the bow, life is perfectly wrapped!" I couldn't. But I could say, "I am seeing God's ways that shine beyond all my hyperventilating ways."

I considered this momentous. Despair-halting decrees rose up.

*What I try not to see is the very thing God will use to set me free.*

*Going with the Spirit means moving with God's wind, not fighting against it.*

*If I believe in the Spirit's possibilities, I will have a chance to see God's incredibility.*

The question we must return to is, will we stay confined or allow ourselves to become redefined? There's probably nothing God wants to do more than to bulldoze the barriers that block confidence and fearlessness so He can push all those little pieces back to hell where they belong.

Where might your mission or your courage be blocked? Where might God want you to take off your shoes? What might that look like?

Take off those shoes that cover your *real*. Let your dirt, your calluses, and your vulnerable self stand bare before God. You aren't too much for Him, I assure you. There are lessons in this place. The place where you bare your feet and bow your head. Don't go distracted or demotivated; expect the Spirit to move on your behalf—to speak your unspeakable. Listen, you tetrachromat.

Things happen in a posture like this. It is not always what we want or how we expect, and not always in a shiny way—but it is always in a far better way, a way that tends to leave us jaw-dropped and feeling flat-out loved.

I picked up the phone and called the health insurance company . . . and the lady said, "You owe nothing."

I already felt like I had gained so much in this lesson. But I guess God had worked some more things out behind the scenes. That is how He works; not always financially but every single time spiritually—in a way that changes us eternally.

After hearing this healthcare news, I broke. In an amazing way, I broke down because the Spirit pressed in a deeper thought: *Even if this bill wasn't paid, you still owe nothing.*

What we owe, Jesus already paid for. What we deserve, we don't get. Our greatest tab is covered. Our insecurities are filled. Our mistakes are not spotlighted. All this stuff, when walked up to the heat of His love, is burned away.

All that lasts is Jesus. Love. Hope personified. A vision that lasts forever.

I wonder, do you know Jesus? I mean, really know Him? If you do, you know hope. If you don't, maybe it is about time you met Him in a more profound way. He died, was buried, and on the third day rose again. He lives. He breathes. He is active. He is everything. He loves you today and every day. There is no need to be fake—or covered. You are the target of His greatest affections. But also, your sin is the target of His greatest wrath when you don't know Him. No joke. A good judge delivers good verdicts. We can't expect anything less, can we? God is good and God is fair.

The problem is that we are human and we really can't stop missing God's standards. You know those, right? Things like: Don't lie. Don't put people down. Don't put things before God.

I miss them all the time. But here is my one hope: Jesus bridges the gap—the gap between my great mess-ups and His super-high standards. If you know Jesus, really know Jesus, you are bound to know real life and real peace. I so badly want you to know Him. I, myself, so badly want to know Him more.

Why do I want this for us? So we don't have to be well-acquainted with pain and warring and despair-laden moments again and again in our lives. And, for some of us, so we don't have to live this way forever. The thought of all that pains me deeply.

I know this all sounds severe, but so does living a life in constant fear and agony. I want us delivered, so I am putting truth on the table with the hope that you can handle it and make the best deal of your life. The Deliverer and Redeemer of all things waits for you—Jesus.

Have you asked Him to be your Savior? Have you really abandoned all to Him? Maybe He is calling you to do it again. He'll be faithful to save. It is His nature; He can't help but do it. He is Deliverer.

If you're ready, pray something like this with me:

*Lord, I can't do it without You. I can't stop messing up. Thank You that You do not abandon me for these things but call me to be Yours. I give all that I am to You. I accept what Christ did for me, how He died and suffered in order to love me. I acknowledge Him as Lord and Savior. I will give my life to serve, love, and follow Him. Amen.*

## Victory Gal

You have to hear about this woman. You might call her a no-holds-barred type. An "I'll show you" gal. A "Bring it! God can do it!" woman, not in an offensive and defensive way but rather in an aggressive and submissive way.

Sound impossible? Read on.

Her name is Deborah. Have you heard of her?

She is called a judge in the Bible, but she is also a counselor, prophetess, and leader. She has courage and initiative and drive and insight and is everything we hope to be, personified in one focused woman. I love her story.

Maybe I love it because I always have wanted to shine. I have always wanted to walk into a room and draw every eye. I have always wanted to command attention and to have people say, "Wow, look at that one. She's got something." I've always wanted that iota of "specialness" that makes us mark someone as being in a different category altogether. My biggest fear is that I don't have "it." That I am just doomed forever to the "average" category.

Deborah didn't just sit there, though. She was the kind of woman you didn't have to actually meet to know, because people wouldn't shush up about her. Why? She was just worthy like that. God blessed her that way.

For one thing, she was the only woman judge, or "special" deliverer, in the time of the Israelites. What an honor. She was chosen by God to be used. She was also decisive, powerful, and influential. For crying out loud, they called this woman the "Mother for Israel" (Judg. 5:7 NLT). Wow. This lady, she shined.

I want to be named something special like her, maybe "Mother for Believers. Mother for Courageous. Mother for Those Who Once Agonized."

The only thing is, this mother had a pending issue, a giant problem—a war headed right toward her. The Canaanites were moving in. Obstacles threatened to take Deborah down.

Now, what does a woman do when she is under attack? She strategizes, of course. She figures out who has the power to make some powerful things happen.

That is exactly what Deborah did. She contacted the general, Barak. The only problem was he was much less "general" and much more, as I see it, "generally anxious." But Deborah saw things differently.

While Barak saw the enemy forces, Deborah saw a great God. While Barak saw "nine hundred chariots fitted with iron [that] had cruelly oppressed the Israelites for twenty years" (Judg. 4:3), Deborah saw victory.

While Barak likely saw his days' end, Deborah likely saw not the end of her days but rather the start of God's new day. The difference between Deborah and Barak is that she believed her King always held the gambit move to change the playing field. She believed in His power to swipe every opponent off the face of the board. She had what is called *faith*. It's the thing that makes little warriors do big things. It's the thing that takes working-class fishermen and makes them into disciples. It's the thing that God will never ask you, upon your arrival in heaven, "Why did you have so much of it?"

Nah, it's the thing that believes if He can, you will. It's the thing that moves mountains and changes hearts and gets the wimpy girls strong. Do you have it?

Deborah did. She was a true mover and shaker, not by her "specialness" but through her reliance on God. Her faith was great and it had the power to remove barriers and enemies—and any ounce of pride that any of this was her own doing.

Deborah called out to Barak, "The LORD, the God of Israel, commands you: 'Go, take with you ten thousand men of Naphtali and Zebulun and lead them up to Mount Tabor. I will lead Sisera, the commander of Jabin's army, with his chariots and his troops to the Kishon River and give him into your hands'" (vv. 6–7).

Half of me wants to rise up and scream, "Yes! Go, girl! You tell him." The other, calmer half of me nods in agreement with her decisive play. It's clear that her godly confidence gives way to good consequences.

Deborah to the rescue!

The Bible doesn't say much about Deborah's doubts. But it seems almost unwomanly not to doubt at all. Maybe she was like me and had some little issues, some little things that needed to be worked out between her and God. I wonder . . . I wonder if, before she gave voice to them, she heard the Spirit's whisper, *Stand down, Deborah.*

Who knows? Maybe her mind was about to lead her wrong but she let her God make things right so her follow-through could be resolute. That thought gives me hope.

"Then Deborah said to Barak, 'Go! This is the day *the* Lord has given Sisera into your hands. Has not *the* Lord gone ahead of you?'" (v. 14, emphasis added).

The Lord goes before you and me too, you know. Do we believe it and proclaim it like Deborah did? She spoke with authority over her problem. She knew her role and was convinced of God's ability to accomplish it.

If only we could be like her, right? To see the bad guys coming. To see the guns blazing and the enemy forces approaching—and to still seek God. To really trust. Not just to say, "I trust when things are easy," but to live trust when things are hard. This is where real faith is.

I want to grab a piece of that. I want to be like Deborah, so doggone confident that I can stand tall like a David meeting a Goliath and walk right up to deliverance—then grab it by the power of God. Deborah did it. She told the general what to do, without showing a slice of doubt of God's instruction. Someone get her a cape, please!

She never let pride get in the way, either, which almost certainly would have been my downfall. Even Barak knew the power of God in her, saying, "If you go with me, I will go; but if you don't go with me, I won't go" (v. 8).

Are we the kind of women people fight to have by their side, or are we too busy trying to run and hide?

Deborah reaches out to me and calls me to emulate her. She calls me to grab the Word of God, follow the leading of the Spirit, and get authoritative—not in a way where I turn all totalitarian or hardened but in a way where I am so tender to God that not following His leading would feel like nails on a chalkboard.

I know what you are thinking right about now, because I am thinking it too: *This all sounds like a tall order. I don't know if I really can do it.*

I guess what I am realizing is that it takes faith to believe in "can" and the knowledge that "God will." But He will, and here is why: first, the Word became flesh and dwelt among us. Then He beat death to reign above us, and now the Spirit has been sent to live in us. The literal and living Spirit of God has moved from outside to inside (1 Cor. 3:16). He is directing (Rom. 8:14), aiding (John 16:13), instructing (1 Cor. 2:10), leading (2 Pet. 1:21), reminding (John 14:26), helping (Acts 9:31), and guiding (Gal. 5:5) us in order to beat every enemy barricade set up against us.

Are we even aware of this internal power? Do we give Him an ounce of credit? Or do we ignore the Spirit as the forgotten God-figure, a vague idea of headship we don't even know?

The Spirit is our confidence.

"Certainly I will go with you," said Deborah. "But because of the course you are taking, the honor will not be yours, for the LORD will deliver Sisera into the hands of a woman" (Judg. 4:9).

Do you notice, like I do, that Deborah was already claiming victory? She said "for the LORD will deliver." When do we speak like this? I sound much more like, "Well, maybe He will . . . I guess He will . . . if He decides to."

No. If God said it is true, He will bring us through. I want to believe like Deborah.

God will help me fear not.

God will be my strength.

God will help me in my time of need.

This is faith that proclaims. It is not a faith designed with the sole purpose of getting your bank account loaded or finding the number-one parking spot or pursuing feel-good moments that usually only leave us over-full and overweight. It is not like that.

This faith helps us stay in the place of believing God will do what He says He will do. What would God tumble down if we confidently spoke His truth with authority?

Women who speak like this don't need machine guns, grenades, or guerilla warfare; they have the leverage of all the legions of God behind them. They simply need the direction and protection of God. Then they can, like Deborah did with the help of warrior-woman Jael, beat down what's coming against them. These women are fiery; it is the fire of the Spirit rising up. And, with this in mind, it comes as no surprise to me that *Deborah* means "fiery woman" in Hebrew.

Let's be modern-day fiery women! What does she look like?

1. **She asks.** She knows if she doesn't know, God does.
2. **She listens.** She knows if she asks, God will answer in some way.
3. **She seeks.** She looks for the enemy's lies to eject them and make room for God's truth.
4. **She waits.** She realizes it's not about her timing but God's best timing.
5. **She acts.** When she knows what is right to do, she does it.
6. **She confidently believes.** She knows God's victory is not a guesstimate but accurate, final, and already won.
7. **She thanks.** She turns back around to those watching and says, "God is good. Look what He did."

A fiery woman is valued, strong, and stable—and she knows it. She doesn't need to fear where she stands, for she knows where she is going. She doesn't need to hate who she was, for God has decided who she is. She doesn't need to focus on death, for she is living in life. She doesn't need to fear the dark, for she carries the light. She walks out, stands before the world, and smiles. Surely she knows that God saves. She speaks and people listen.

But make no mistake, living like this fiery woman is a choice, a decision, and a declaration.

It's far less about having shiny circumstances or a picture of a sparkling future or an image with no cracks and much more about the small choice to remove your shoes in faith, knowing God is planning goodness for you.

So lean back, take off your shoes, and get comfortable, for this new, vivid perspective, derived from all things Spirit, is about to radically revive your life.

## Something to Chew On

**A Sayonara to Fear** (Speak aloud and own these words in your life): Fear, I want to address you. It has been nice knowing you. It has been nice because you are familiar, known ground. But, still, you have been an enemy standing in front of my Promised Land—one that God desires I fully enter into. I will no longer stand on shifting ground where my body trembles at the thought of judgments, progress, perfection, worries, control, anxieties, or worst-case scenarios. If God delivered the Israelites after forty years of wandering, He can surely be faithful to me too. So, today, I inch toward the start of goodbye to you. I wave a white flag to God and a victory flag over stagnation. Cheers, fear.

# *three*
# Discovering Super Spirit

> I am building a fire, and every day I train, I add more fuel. At just the right moment, I light the match.
>
> Mia Hamm

*D*id you know people take longer to move their cars when another car is waiting?[1] Did you know that people are more likely to eat fatty foods when the labels prove they shouldn't?[2] Did you know that the more parents plead against teenage relationships, the more their sweet Romeo and Juliet want each other? No wonder this desire is actually called the Romeo and Juliet effect.[3]

What we know we shouldn't do—we do. The apple we know is restricted—we bite it. This mentality is as old as Adam: "When the woman saw that the fruit of the tree was good for food and pleasing to the eye, and also desirable for gaining wisdom, she took some and ate it" (Gen. 3:6).

We almost can't help ourselves. It tastes good. It looks good. We reach and we bite. Food. I love to love it and I love to hate it, as you will later come to see.

Chocolate is my favorite. When I see it my eyes light up. If you were to place a tray of succulent, chocolate-covered strawberries before me and tell me not to eat them, let me tell you, I'd attack them the minute you were out the door. I don't care what you told me. Nothing comes between me and my sugar fix.

I want it. I eat it.

How often do you, like me, ignore what you should do and indulge in what you shouldn't?

We call that person. We head to that area. We hide our stuff. We look at that page. We speed. We take those office supplies. We talk to that person. We park in that spot. We think those thoughts.

What do you tend to do?

I am a prime example of this. If my husband gives me detailed ideas on how we're going to approach something, guess what happens? I ignore them. Not only that, but I put my spin on them.

You want to go that direction? Oh, no; not that way, I know a better way. You want a pizza restaurant? Nah. We really should get Italian. Poor guy.

It doesn't end there for us humans. "Keep off the grass" means "cut the corner." "Don't worry" means "keep on thinking about how you worry, and then start to worry about that." "Chill out" means "get stressed because you are not chill."

Part of me can't help but do what I am not supposed to do, and I am not so sure how to change. All I know is something pretty super is required to help me.

## The Reactance Theory

Thank goodness there is a whole theory based around this dissension, because otherwise I'd really feel lousy. But there is (thank you, God); it is called the Reactance Theory. This theory demonstrates that when people feel rule-controlled, they take control.

For instance, researcher Daniel Wegner told people not to think of a cuddly white bear.[4] He pretty much told the group, "Keep it out of your mind, and don't let it in." But guess just what they did?

You got it. They couldn't get it off their minds. They thought about those bears two times more than the group that was never told to restrain their thinking.

We just want to do what we want to do; it is our nature. We don't want to lose. A lot of it comes down to this: we're deathly afraid that if we don't take charge, someone else will. So we defend ourselves. We overexert ourselves. *Must. Not. Lose. Power.*

In what areas are you deathly afraid life will charge over you and leave you for dead?

I envision our little defiances like personal strikes, where we bounce signs up and down and chant, "I know best. I know best. I know best. Don't boss me. Don't boss me. Don't boss me." With each phrase, we get louder and louder, until everyone wants to run away.

I can't lie to myself—I do this with God too. He tells me to "fear not" over three hundred times in the Bible, and guess what I do? I fear. He tells me to trust. Guess what I do? I doubt. Ugh. I wish I didn't. But I really do. Do you?

How do we do what God tells us to do rather than living by doing what we are trying not to do? (Is your mind as twisted up by all this as mine is?)

Or is this simply a latte too tall to drink?

I wonder. Because when I hear "Don't worry," I have to face the fact that I have chosen to worry for just about my whole life. It goes like this: *Where is my husband? He should be home by now. He always is. I shouldn't worry about it. I know I am not supposed to worry about it. He's going to be home soon. Stop worrying; watch TV. I said stop thinking about it, he is fine. Don't you dare text him, he's driving. I wonder if he got my text? He'd better not get in an accident looking at it. If he doesn't get home soon I am calling someone. Kelly, stop pacing.*

(Door swings open. Husband enters.)

"How dare you not let me know you were okay?! You don't know what I went through. Be more considerate next time," I say.

"Didn't I mention I was going to be home fifteen minutes late?" he says.

Whoops! I guess I shouldn't have worried.

How can we stop doing what we don't want to do (Rom. 7:15; James 4:17) so that we can actually start doing what God wants us to do? Loving others. Honoring them. Forgiving. Obeying. Trusting. Believing.

Is it all futile, or can God really give us a new ability? All I know is that I need some sort of super-ability to fix my deficiencies. Can God help us? Let's see.

## Considering a New Thing

I really hate to say this, friends, because talking about this kind of stuff is kind of equivalent to pulling out those bags of brand-new clothes you've hidden in your closet to keep secret from your loved one, but, still, I am going to.

I am going to drag those expensive bags out and lay them before you, so you can see all I am trying to hide. What do you have hidden in the dark corners, figuring no one can see? I am not trying to be cruel when I ask you this, I promise you. And when you give me the evil eye that says, *You are capable of making me feel that guilty?* I am just going to look at you, with a half smirk, and say, *Well, yes, I am.*

Underneath it all, I feel horrible about my stuff. I do. Embarrassed. For sure. I see my own mess. Plus, I know—you and me—we hide because we feel bad. That is why we do it. We just can't leave all that visible.

But what I am coming to see, and the reasoning behind my smirk, is that this horrible feeling—the regret, the remorse, the shame, the guilt, the self-reproach—is not as bad as we Christians think. Even though I try to fend it off, run from it, and hide it deep, deep back in a corner, this feeling is actually used by God.

It proves He loves me, that He is not pulling away from me. It confirms I am His.

It's kind of like a daddy bringing his child to the doctor for shots. He or she experiences pain, but he allows it because in the long run he wants his beloved child safe, protected, and vaccinated against future illness.

God often lets us go through pain so we will press in to His love. We get an injection of conviction, and upon reflection we uncover His protection. God shows up, because be it spiritual or physical wellness, the Great Physician can't help but heal.

Now, if only I can believe, in the moment, that He has my best interests in mind. It is hard to see in the moment. It really is. But looking at that feeling of guilt, seeing it for what it is, and nodding at it actually gets us somewhere. Beyond that, the words "I am sorry, God. Please help me" move us even further. They make the difference between just inching along and express training, I think.

I just think about my son. When he says "Sorry," eyes averted and face tilted down, I am certain things won't change much. But when he looks me eye to eye and says, "Oh, Mommy, I did wrong. I am so sorry," I become certain we have made progress.

When we get really sorry, the Spirit gets really powerful inside us. In this space humility creates within us, He works. And when He does we feel new insight and motivations rise up.

Guilt isn't an emotion you cover your ears and run from—it is one you listen for.

Because God loves you, He will be faithful to discipline you (Heb. 12:6). So, let's remember: we are not bad because we feel bad. This feeling is a signal, much like the final bell at school; the Spirit uses it to signal to His children that it is time to look for Daddy.

Are we looking for Daddy when that alarm of guilt, self-reproach, and condemnation goes off? These feelings are not our enemy; they are our wakeup call that we're about to get a great rescue from a great Daddy.

Rescue us, Daddy! We need Your help!

Daddy's here to help. He wants to send us out in the right way to go. He put the Spirit inside us to help us with this. You see, the Spirit is His specialist. He points out all our little wrongs to bring in a renewed way of thinking, acting, and doing (John 16:8). It is not so we can become routine-driven robots of poised perfection but so we can react to the tender motions of a God who is always moving.

He primes us so He can paint us with His glory.

He assures us so we can know love.

He tells truth so we can live free.

In many regards, it boils down to this:

*My ways + my thoughts = frustration, irritation, and the consequences of sin*

*God's new ways + my surrendered heart = a courageous, bold, Spirit-led life*

Let's not run from what we have always run from, or tell ourselves just to plain ol' stop. The best thing to do is move into something new. Let's do this in such a way that all we hear is:

- The Lord is with me; I will not be afraid. What can anyone do to me? (Ps. 118:6)
- God is my help and shield. (Ps. 115:11)
- I can be strong and courageous. God goes with me; He will never leave me nor forsake me. (Josh. 1:9)
- But from everlasting to everlasting the Lord's love is with me; because I fear Him, His righteousness is with me. (Ps. 103:17)
- Praise the Lord. I am blessed and delight in Him. (Ps. 112:1)

Do you see what I see? With words like this resonating within us, there is no place for "Get over it, girls," "Stop its," "Quit thats," or "You can'ts." They are rendered ineffective. We let go of all we are not and see all that God is.

We don't need to tell ourselves to stop because the Spirit says *Start*. Start fearing God rather than fearing that everyone is going to take you down. It is a shift that works, because when we are filled with God it doesn't leave room for much else.

It all boils down to this: the Super Spirit is at work doing a new thing for those tired of their old things.

It's not a whole lot of lecturing; it's not a whole lot of stops— "Stop that fearing, you bad child. Stop messing up. Stop being lame." Nope, it is a different word. It is the word *start*. Start perceiving something new. Something different. Life-giving. Breath-inducing.

What is your "start"? The Spirit will be faithful to help it emerge as you submerge those old desires under the heights of God's love.

Sure, you may be in a wilderness. Sure, you may feel wasted in a wasteland. Sure, you may feel parched, scorched, and dying for a fresh drink, but did you hear?

Listen to this: "See, I am doing a *new thing*! Now it springs up; do you not perceive it? I am making *a way in the wilderness* and *streams in the wasteland*" (Isa. 43:19, emphasis added).

The Super Spirit is doing something with super-amazing results!

He is making a way. A way to hope. A way to life. A way to go. A way to breathe. A way out of desperation. A way past discouragement. A way of less doubt.

Choose to perceive it.

Streams in a wasteland: a fresh drink. Life-giving sustenance. Beauty. Renewal.

A *new thing* looks like this:

Negating

Every

Worthless

Thing
Hindering the
I AM's
Next
Great Act

I Am. You know who He is, right? He's the One who exists everywhere, at all times, and in every way. He's Father, Son, and Holy Spirit. That One—He is up to something new. It is not about law-keeping but all about becoming God-pleasing. That's how the new thing shows up; He works His way to the door the Super Spirit just pressed open.

It's never about shame; it's all about gain. Let Him in. Uncross your arms, settle your breathing, relax, and grab these despair-halting decrees that speak life:

*Conviction is a revelation that brings deeper interpretation.*

*Listening to the Spirit's direction brings godly connection.*

*When you become undone in godly adoration, you won't become undone in self-condemnation.*

### Perfect Love Drives Out Outlandish Fear

I remember when I was just a seven-year-old girl. Insecure, unsure, and looking for more, I dreamed of a time when my future fantasies would become reality.

Lying in the grass, discerning the shapes of the clouds and my future, I would often ask, "God, do you see me? Do you care?"

I couldn't really put God to the test, so I would put the test on my parents. I would ask myself, *How long will it take them to come running when I start screaming bloody murder? Will my pain make them more likely to see me?*

Then I would do it. I would scream from the bottom of my lungs, fear-curdling screams.

I just wanted to be seen. Seen by the kids who laughed at my hair. Seen by the ones who were too cool for me. Seen by the teacher who thought I was dumb. Seen by the God who seemed to be up in the clouds. Seen for who I truly was.

Seen by someone—almost anyone.

I dreamed of escape, of possibility—of King Kong–like scaling abilities and having neon-green energized fluids that would make me super. My refuge was the idea of being a super girl, with super skills, who would grow up one day to be a super woman. A woman who did things beyond herself. One who lived life with super strength, ran at super speed, and flew high with super powers. Super enemies, of course, would be no obstacle for this girl because her bright light would blind the opposition.

I loved this super girl because she wasn't me—an ordinary girl. When I pretended to be her, I was indestructible, unwavering, and incredible. I ran untouched. I was better than myself.

I have always longed to know her. I have always dreamt of her. I have always aspired to reach these kinds of heights.

But what do you do when God shuts down a dream? When everything you ever hoped you would be is shattered right before your very eyes?

All grown up, I crossed a busy Chicago street one windy day and my vision was changed—literally.

My eyes could no longer focus. They couldn't see the line of cars headed toward me. They couldn't even see my next step. They couldn't see my destination in the midst of the bustling city. All they could see was my world through distorted prisms of black and white. I stumbled. I was losing my sight—and all I had ever known, all at the same time. Suddenly, my loss of vision proved my destructibility: I was breaking down, and there was nothing I could do. I knew then that I clearly wasn't super . . . and I clearly was super uncared for too.

I survived the next few months with numb legs and a numb heart. My condition was a constant reminder that I could never escape the shell of that faulted little girl.

My cape of hope lost power. Replacing it was a mask of insecurity adorned with an "I-trust-Jesus" smile. Yet behind this mask I was convinced the world was about to eat me up and overtake me. It was going to steal my dream of a life that mattered. It would make me feel more alone than ever. It would hinder the blessing of relationship and crush all hope of a future.

My mind played on silent repeat: *I am not valuable. I am unworthy. I deserve to be sick.*

I didn't sign up for this kind of defeatist life. I had other plans. Not these plans. Not ones that made me hospital-bound. Not plans of agony. Not plans of despair. Not plans where I couldn't even see how I was supposed to get up and fight. These were not my plans.

When the doctors finally muttered the words *multiple sclerosis*, my heart stopped—dead. Well, almost. In an instant, I knew then that I would never be a super girl, just super disappointed with my lot in life.

What do you do in this place? When you feel entirely useless? Incapable?

Pain surrounded me. Bills mounted. Troubles didn't cease.

Hope appeared to be a cloud: apparent for a moment—gone the next.

I was angry.

God had walked out on me. He'd given up on helping me out. He wasn't listening. Or so I thought.

Naturally, with Him absent, I started thinking about myself a whole lot. And isn't that how it is with fear? It is a song of self that belts out "I am going to die and no one is here to save me."

I doubted. *God, surely You don't rescue girls with nothing left to give.*

I had nothing left to offer. I was depleted. And I don't know—but looking back, perhaps this is just where God wanted me to be. It is the point of giant faith leaps.

When we have nothing left to give, we quickly realize we have everything to gain. We unlatch the limiting harness of striving and trust God to carry us through to thriving. We approach the unscalable and climb with His hand on our back. We let go. We see from different perspectives. We start to see *super*.

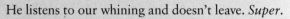

He listens to our whining and doesn't leave. *Super.*

He pacifies our jagged nerves pressed right into Him. *Super.*

He shields us from the rain of condemnation. *Super.*

He requires no performance, show, or dance. *Super.*

*Super* lets you feel like you don't have to spend your whole life trying to be.

I let loose some pride that day. It felt good. I felt super.

It looked like this: *God, You have me here for a reason. You are great, mighty, and know what is best; I fear You. Let me go as You go and move as You move.*

As I grabbed hold of this, my own loss of myself felt less like loss and more like loved. I stopped fearing as much and started fearing God.

Do you fear God—living life in awe, in anticipation, and in adventure? Not fearing Him in a way where you get all shaky and nervous and defensive, but in a way where God moves into position number-one. In a way where He gets to stand above everything else you fear.

Why is this so important? Because seeing that He can do it all, be it all, and exist in every category helps you realize you'll be okay, and that His plans always win. This helps me. It might help you too.

Sure, it's risky; but usually risky is where courage is forged.

How did it turn out for me? God answered. He placed me right next to a woman struggling with bone cancer in a waiting room.

Talk about putting things into perspective! Her sullen face showed her discouragement. Her hunched shoulders spoke eloquently of the excruciating pain she was living in. Her words expressed how she would have to endure this her whole life. There was no escaping her torture; absolutely nothing could be done. Her meds wouldn't work. She longed for the day that would be her last.

My heart broke. *How can I save her?* I thought.

I only wish I could. I so often wish I could save the hurting ones.

But, in that moment, I noticed something else. I noticed I felt something, well, *super*. A super push? A super inkling? A super prompting? Call it what you will, but it rose up in me, in that teeny space of a waiting room; it was an inclination that seemed to force me beyond my comfort zone with the words, *Kelly, less of you. More of Me* (John 3:30).

While in any other moment I would have shoved aside *super* for worried, anxious, and annoyed (after all, I also was waiting to get a sound-blaring, needle-protruding MRI), this moment ended up different. This moment was like a sparkler set off in the dark. In my frail condition, I saw a hurting soul and we both saw Jesus as we leaned in, together, no longer trapped in the cell of a windowless waiting room but united. Prayer rose up from two sorry, skinny, scared, and only-surviving souls, and what we got was renewal.

She experienced hope and I saw the first glimmer of "fear fighter" in me. Some corner of real red cape emerged, even if it looked like a hospital gown. But I knew—this *super* wasn't me. *Super* was Super Spirit.

What might Super Spirit forge if only we surrender our plans and follow His? Might He unveil our inadequacies not as disabilities but as opportunities?

Think of a sponge. Some might say the holes make it weird looking; I say the holes make it capable of absorbing life—and holding it. The Spirit makes our holes, our oddness, purposeful. He saturates us with God.

I want to love me a little more. I want to run back to me, that seven-year-old girl, grab hold of her shoulders, look into her sullen and scared eyes, and tell her, "Sweet one, please know: you are seen, so seen. Put on your cape again; keep hope. Super God is giving you power. Just believe, grab hold, and fly where He flies. By His might, you're bound to end up okay."

I might even hand her "super" binoculars and say, "When it darkens, keep looking up and you won't get so panicked by all that's around." I would want her to see hope.

After that, I might motion her to look toward God one final time, whispering, "You might even get surprised, for He's not far. He is right with you and all around you."

That would have been nice. Tidy. Comforting. Something only I could say to me and understand enough to grab hold of.

But some things just have to be learned; they have to be forged through iron and nit and grit. They have to be figured out without instructions, so that God has the honor of instructing all the way through. It's how He designed it, after all. So, maybe, going back, I'd leave her untouched but just offer a little wink, saying, "You'll make it through; just cling to that."

Do we cling to that? That our Super God will really bring us through? I think the Spirit has some little whispers He wants that little you to know. Can you hear them? Have you asked? What things might you whisper to that younger you?

So, my MRI? How did that end up? You'd probably never consider that loud-sounding tube a house of prayer, but that is exactly what it became. With the weight of my new friend on my shoulders and a promise to pray for her, all I could do was settle in and pray. In fact, I became so relaxed and in tune with God that the doctors actually questioned me to find out what was wrong. Uh, no, I wasn't in a trance or passed out, I was just having a heart-to-heart chat with Super Spirit in the presence of a very real God. I met with *peace*. Fortunately, this moment of peace, and probably one thousand prayers, changed my diagnosis too, which landed me at more peace.

> Sometimes God heals us physically. Often He heals us emotionally. But nearly every time, through trials, He heals us spiritually, and no matter what, we will all be healed in eternity.

So let's not doubt the extraordinary and indispensable powers of the Spirit. He is real, very real—and that little presence in you is not small. He is gigantic in power, power that is regenerative in its abilities. He is far bigger than even your largest conception of Him. He is extraordinary; He is (dun, dun, dun) Super Spirit, after all!

## New Super You

God is calling us to a great birth—a birth that may look different than we ever expected but far better. He is growing and nourishing newness, even when we can't see it and even when we can't believe it—so that one day, when our labor pains end, what we end up with, what we hold in our hands, ends up undoing our heart with a newfound ability to love.

And what we know in that moment, our only moment, is that we stand in the center of wild opportunity and life. So we look around, perhaps pinch ourselves. Maybe we even jump a tad, because what we know now and become certain of is that we are *really alive*. And yes, it is scary, but it is also good, because finally we are certain we're just a little more on track to where we were meant to go. We are finally getting somewhere.

This new birth opens up new hope.

> We no longer see religious demands or commands,
> the waves that are far too big,

overwhelming failures,
shame,
or inadequacies . . .
we see life.
Vision, destiny, and love wait on the horizon.

We return to new, unafraid to admit our wrongs. We look and we see what we never believed possible—super things forged by a Super Spirit.

## *Something to Chew On*

**Awakening Courage:** *Awaken, dear child; awaken and see. Awaken to eagerness, to anticipation, and to expectancy. Surely we will ride to new heights and voyage through new lows, but together we will go. You will ride under My wing of hope. As we move, your fretting will be exchanged for freedom. The lows will be exchanged for highs. Depression will be exchanged for pure expression. Your eyes will see like never before. The wind will release you in the direction you should go. In the here and now, we will see, feel, experience, learn, and move as one. You and Me—there is no room for uncertainty because you are certain of where you lie, under a protected wing that shields you. It shields you under the shadow of love, under the covering of My arm and the distance I can bring you. Come, dear child; oh, the places we will go.*

We don't have to see it all to be fearless; we just have to fear the One who does.

# Part 2

# Spirit Arising

## Demolishing
## the Eight Fear-Inducers

*four*

# The Devil

## Smothering Power

Joy runs deeper than despair.

Corrie ten Boom

*Is tonight going to be the night? Is it going to happen again? Will it be yet another time where I am eaten alive, nearly swallowed whole, and then spit out like last week's garbage? Will I again be prey to yet another attack? What if he comes? Is that a shadow?*

Her body can't help but clench up in raw fear. It is heart-wrenching fear. Agonizing fear. Have you ever felt that moment?

My dear friend Neena lived this torture nearly every day, because the moving shadows weren't just figments of her imagination—they were real. She couldn't sleep; closing her eyes was too risky. Instead, chest thumping, mind running, muscles tight, she kept her eyes wide open on high alert. She had to. She never knew when he would come and what she could do to save herself.

What do you do when your reality of fear appears much closer than any probability that God is near? When you can nearly feel, hear, and smell it breathing down your neck?

It stood over Neena. It always did.

As a child, Neena was cradled and then bottle-fed to sleep with rum. She was thrown down so hard her shoulder was dislocated. She was laughed at and ridiculed by her mom. She was tossed up in the air, giggles and all, only to land with a parental figure's hand clenching her private area. Pain was her life and loneliness her agenda, and the doors out were locked. Disillusionment ruled her house.

How do we rise up when what is pressing down on us seems like it wants to kill us?

My friends, let's pause right here so I can put my arm around you and say something, woman to woman. What I am about to say may shock you; it may stop you or threaten your normal thinking, but I have to say it: there is a real enemy against us, and if we don't get fighting he'll start knocking our emotional and spiritual well-being to the ground.

You see, he roams around all hot and bothered, especially by those women who are or will be daughters of God. We, as giant threats to his domain, really make his face red. (I can nearly imagine it growing bigger and hotter, can't you?) He wants to get his hands all over us. Will it always look as extreme as Neena's situation? No. But will it tend to feel horrible and raw and painful and disconcerting when it appears in our lives? Almost always, yes.

Are you aware of him? He prowls around in the dark, seeking little girls in big girls' bodies to devour (1 Pet. 5:8). What hurt years ago he wants to keep pin-pricking today. He wants to keep forcing you to remember how damaged, how deplorable, and how disposable you really are.

The devil wants you to relive past trauma every day—every moment, if he can make you. He wants you to spend your whole life running from you, that hurt little girl, rather than bringing her right up to the love of Jesus.

*Run, girl, run! Don't look back, just keep going!*

We women, we are busy. We are mostly doers. We are day-makers. We are work-forgers. We are lovers. We take care of others. We are head-down in an iPhone. We are routine drivers. We are planners and strategists. We are trying our best, but we often are hardly thinking about an enemy attacker ready to besiege us.

In some ways, I want to clap my hands and wake us all up! Just because you can't see him lurking behind your shrubs doesn't mean he isn't there. He is. He's slitherin' and slimin' around us, hoping to devour holy. He is no joke. Sometimes what you can't see really can hurt you. He is evil incarnate and the summation of everything horrible, and the devil is after you.

Do I want you paranoid? No. Do I want you aware? Yes, with the goal that you will raise your head so you can raise your God higher as you keep your heart set on Him.

How do you tell if you have been targeted? If you spend your life circling self-hatred and shame, you can be quite sure the devil's pulled some strings.

He's done it to me. So many times. And this I have learned: the tables start to shift when I call out his game. We can see things for what they are and say, "There he goes again. You aren't going to catch me this time, you little sneak." We can call out his intention to steal, kill, and destroy (John 10:10) and replace it with Jesus's plan—to heal, fill, and redeploy.

It makes all the difference. I want to get wise like this, don't you?

Because the one we listen to is the one we're prone to follow. If we can't hear truth, we won't follow it. And if we only hear lies, we'll live by them. What voice do you tend to hear—the voice of God or the voice of evil? The voice of self or the voice of God?

Let's take a pop quiz: Do any of these beliefs play out in your mind?

1. I am no better than my past. It is bound to repeat.
2. I will become just like the one who most hurt me. It is already happening.

3. I will never feel better. I will always be lonely, sad, and _____.

4. God will never do great things for me; I am not like those other people.

5. I am a hopeless cause. I'd better act perfect so no one knows.

6. People (including God) run from people like me. I look like a (fat, ugly, dumb) mess. I will never be good enough for anyone.

7. I will always be alone. I can't trust anyone else, either.

8. God can't be near those who are as bad as me. I can't be forgiven.

9. I will never be good enough. I keep on failing.

10. God won't really come through for me.

This is often the voice of the devil (sometimes mixed with our voice of self), my friends. If the devil can't completely devastate us from the outside-in, he'll work to decimate us from the inside-out. It's fact.

Here's another filter to help identify the voice you hear:

1. If it woos with the voice of love, it is God.

2. If it calls you closer to God (through a message of repentance, forgiveness, and always-available mercy), it is God.

3. If it speaks truth (Scripture, life, biblical liberty), it is God.

4. If it wants to beat you, tie you, and throw you out back for always being despicable, I assure you, it is not God. Anything not founded in love does not equal God.

## Outside In

Are you at all like me? If one bad thing happens, I am okay. Two things? I start to get frustrated. But three horrible things? I turn into a hot mess of frustration where the whole world seems to be working against me. It is at this point I figure that I will never make it out alive, that I am bound to fail, that traffic lights turn red because they hate me, and that I can never do things right. It is right about at this point of agitation that anger, wrath, and vileness can't help but gush out onto all those around me.

I am convinced this kind of thing, in part, is the strategy of the devil. I think he knows my ways. He knows, "Keep pinging her and you will eventually get to her." I can't help but notice something, though; I am the one who signs off on this faulty agreement with him. Sure, he can send trials, but he can't force me to act like a lunatic. I raise my hand for that on my own. I choose that reaction.

The truth is, he has no power to break my insides unless I let his power in. Too often I grant permission. I sign on the dotted line and say, "You got me. We have a deal." Then I start self-protecting, self-defending, demanding, power-playing, and the like. I wish I would just keep him cold, hungry, and stuck outside the door of my mind. Then I wouldn't have to work so hard to break out of his fault-filled contracts.

The problem is, I don't. I give him access to walk right into my office, my sorting place. I hand him a cup of coffee, saying, "Make yourself at home." We hang out and talk about all the dumb things I do. I listen to all of his pointed accusations. I look down at my feet and feel beaten down. And then, like the horrible lawyer he is, he usually scares me senseless and makes me doubt the very fabric of everything God declares me to be until I am convinced, head nodding, I will fail, fall, or forget about God—which I inevitably do.

Our sign-off on a lie-filled agreement is our greatest impediment to abundant life (John 10:10). We put into motion a course of action we never wanted. The damages are horrible.

Discouragement is the agreement to self-inflict punishment. Doubt is the agreement to circumvent faith.

Despair is the agreement that God isn't fair.

Devastation is the agreement that money, power, beauty, sex, and pleasure are life's foundation.

Damages are things that fill the void left by the lies that seemingly stole God's goodness.

Am I trying to scare you? Nah. I just want us to be aware. I want to shock us awake to the reality of what we don't realize is happening. But I also want you to know you don't have to live in fear.

Jesus is the only agreement that stands up in the court of God's law. You see, Jesus is both Judge (John 5:22) and Advocate (Heb. 7:25); He is always pleading and interceding on our behalf. The decks are stacked; our Lord is the greatest defender and protector who ever lived and Satan has no chance of winning when we allow Jesus to work for us.

In this, I don't really care what agreements any of us have intentionally or unintentionally signed off on. These kinds of contracts—they are moot when they come against the blood, mercy, and hope of Jesus Christ. When we turn toward the heart of God we get cleaned up in His midst; lies can't stand in the face of His love. Never. Ever.

Jesus won this case. There is no stupid, dumb, or horrendous act we can ever commit that can cause a retrial. The only question is, will we let His truth stand—as truth? Will we believe it is so established that any kind of rebuttals and retorts sent to throw us off are false? Will we see the future that has already been revealed and remember there is no way Jesus can't win?

For one day Jesus will ride in on a white horse, our rescuing knight. His eyes will resemble fire and His head will wear many crowns, and we will see the name that stands above all names (Rev. 19:12). His immensity will likely stagger us. And what will come? The devil will lose. He, and everything horrible he brought with him, will be thrown into the sea of torment all day, every day—and for eternity more (20:10).

This plan is established and is more permanent than your physical body. Jesus and His followers belong together. Always and forever. That is truth. That is security. No scheme of hell can separate us—ever (Rom. 8:38–39). Not under any condition. Not under any mindset. Not now. Not ever. May we always remember this, because holding on to this truth is the equivalent of a power-punch delivered straight between our opponent's eyes. *Bam!*

Now, some of you may look at me and say, "Well, Kelly, that all sounds fine and dandy, but Jesus is long gone. He can't really help me in the here and now, when everything hits me with the force of a nuclear bomb."

I hear you, and thank you for your honesty, but let me remind you of something else, my friend: He who is in us cannot be touched by he who is not (1 John 4:4). The Spirit is cocooned safely within the sacred walls of God's blessed temple, you, and He can't be injured, erased, or deleted from inside us (1 Cor. 3:16).

Still not sinking in?

No evil can work when holiness surrounds.
No arrows can penetrate when the Spirit dominates.
No accusations can debilitate when holiness is activated.

This Spirit cuddles against our heart, and He is the wellspring of life (Prov. 4:23) and its protector (Rom. 8:2).

If you set your mind on the constant and indestructible One in you, versus the turbulence around you, you'll find both peace and life (vv. 5–6). These two things are found through a mind set on all things Spirit, not flesh, not evil, not wars—but Spirit. They are also found by the new covenant—or contract—loaded with the unmerited favor worked out by Jesus (continual mercy, love, and forgiveness). The details look permanent, irreversable, and irrevocable. The clauses and paragraphs mark us as kingdom-carriers, temple-keepers, and God-warriors—even when our mind tries to negotiate otherwise.

Jesus paid the price and that deal is done.

## A Quick Pause (Put on Your Listening Ears)

Issues, bills, people problems, waiting games—you name it, these stinkers have been after me lately. They've been known to send me into a fetal position and evoke a few tears, but usually, after I finally get my zebra face wiped off, I get to thinking. Can I blame everything on the devil? No way. Some things are me, the results of my desires and inclinations, and some things are just beyond my understanding. However, in some cases it is the devil. And while he wants to ruin us with circumstances, the Spirit wants to remake us by them. The devil will sometimes send a whole bunch of things to attack, but he can never steal Christ in us, our hope of glory (John 16:14–15; Col. 1:27). The Spirit in me is constant, so I don't have to live constantly anxious. Even if life tumbles, the Spirit-thread in me, like my DNA, cannot be unwoven. And what I can be sure of is even if circumstance after circumstance crumbles and tumbles, day after day, I can rest confidently that I am being shaken loose to be re-formed into the image of Christ. Imagine that! If I looked like Him, I might look like peace, calm, courage, power, and strength. I want it. I want all that. I want Him. Steady footing.

This kind of talk is what returns sanity; it returns us to reality, which every time is God, by the way. It is the voice of love, speaking like this: *My child, I am your Abba Daddy* (Rom. 8:15). *Wait for Me, take courage, and then you will be strong* (Ps. 27:14).

God basically says, *Start holding My hand of courage in the face of your fears.*

And, somehow, this message works. For after you wail and whine, you somehow begin to know when the voice of the Spirit is speaking. You become confident you *can*, and you *will*. So you pack up all the ugly Ds—doubt, discouragement, devastation, and despair—and you send them packing.

You have places to go with God. You grab His hand and whisper, "Let's go."

## The Alternative

*I will end it*, she decided. And she tried. Neena downed a bottle of pills—and failed. And, without God, nearly every time after failure comes punishment.

Pain was inflicted on her in all sorts of ways. Ways unimaginable. Ways indescribable in a book like this. Everyone involved needed to be absolved of their own pain; Neena was the punching bag.

Need to relieve your stress? Neena.

Angry? Neena.

On a verbal tirade? Neena.

*You're a laughingstock! Despicable and disgusting. A loser. A failure, a shame, a mockery of a woman. No one will ever love you, Neena. You'll lose! You want pain. Worthless girl!*

Abiding by the voice of lies leads to demise. Neena found herself high on sex, hardened by pain, aggravated by life, a mother at age fifteen, and walking with gut-wrenching remorse from bad decisions. Pain became known. Fear became friendly. Bruises became larger. Controllers more controlling. Abuse was emboldened. The devil gained mindshare. Neena discovered witchcraft. Life became a war. Days became a battle—one she desperately couldn't figure out how to fight, let alone win.

Until one day at home, without warning, her boyfriend pressed a gun against her head. He said, "If I can't have you, no one will. I am killing you, the baby, and myself."

She thought, *Anything is better than this hell on earth. It will be easy.* And she dared him to pull the trigger.

Easy doors often lead to hard consequences. Do you take easy doors out?

It's easy to look at Neena and think, *I am not like her. I am in my safe little suburban home; I am shielded, armed, and protected from this kind of nonsense. This stuff happens to others but not me, not on my manicured yard, with my two little pets and my picket fence. Nope. I don't look for easy doors out of pain like she did.*

Let me draw you near and whisper something to you, fear friend: I know I am much like you, but guess what? We are listening to lies again. You and me, no doubt, we seek easy doors out, just like Neena did, all the time. Let's ask the Holy Spirit to awaken us to truth. Maybe we walk through a door of excuses that could shut down the life of our marriage. A door of rationalization that lets us keep talking to the boyfriend of old on Facebook. A door of wine that is only meant to take the edge off a hard day, except it happens (times two glasses) every single night. A door of overspending that threatens to make us lose our house to foreclosure. A door of potato chips that at least isn't as bad as the pan of brownies we ate yesterday. A door of anger that we use when we really need our kids to shut up. A door of hiding when we don't want to see that person we can't forgive. A door we shut on friends because we figure they'll never really love us.

We each have doors. They are the ones we tend to leave propped wide open for easy access. They are the ones we escape to. And the devil can usher us right up and through them—hardly noticed.

What is your easy door? What could it be, if left unguarded?

Pick it and find out what's behind it later, right? Door #1 leads us to regret. Door #2 leads us to embarrassment. Door #3 leads us to pain. Door #4 leads us to hide. Door #5 leads us to fear.

Are you seeing a pattern yet? There is only one true door—and His name is Jesus (John 10:7). He's the only entry to enduring goodness.

### Spirit, Stat!

Sometimes knowing what you don't want proves what you do. Of course, we don't want doors that lead us to self-hatred. That is a given. We don't want fear that gives way to greater fear. That is for sure. We don't want to listen to lies that encourage us to lie. Been there, done that.

What we do want is the Spirit who brings kingdom-come. We want the Spirit who is our promise keeper. We want a lantern of hope to shine in us, around us, and through us—in a way where God floodlights and blinds the devil.

Yes, certainly, we want all this. We want it really bad. We want it simply and quickly, and we want to grab it—like a pile of gifts on our birthday. We say, "Yes, I'll take all this good stuff for me."

Yet part of us says, "Sounds good; in theory this is all fine and dandy and nicely gift-wrapped, but *how*?" How do we prevent our earthly shells from becoming shellacked by the shame-maker? And what do we do when everything does combust, like when:

A marriage disintegrates faster than your good looks?

A medical issue keeps your brain tied in knots?

A bank account looks as small as last year's bikini?

An addiction can't be halted?

A drinking problem threatens ruin?

An ex-husband starts dating again?

A child shoots drugs?

A mind just won't hold on to truth?

The list goes on and on, and so do our days and our chances of meeting pain. We need a plan, right? That is how I feel. How does the saying go? "Failing to plan is planning to fail." I guess I agree: I am so over failing. Are you?

If so, here's a daily plan to fight the enemy. It will help—I hope.

### 1. Spirit Plead (Ask)

Asking the Spirit for help might sound like this prayer, based on Ephesians 6:14–17.

> *God, I submit to You. I lay it all down. I am weak, so be strong for me. Give life to all the places where I feel dead.*

*I want to put on the full armor of God so that I can stand firm against the strategies and tricks of the devil; help me to do this.*

*I put on the breastplate of righteousness that reminds me: in You, I am good. I hold tight to my belt of truth, which means I put every thought through the filter of Your promises before I accept it.*

*I stand with the shoes of the gospel that walk peace right into my heart, peace that knows Jesus understands and saves me minute by minute. I wear the helmet of salvation and know that my place as daughter in Your great kingdom can never be erased. I yield the sword of the Spirit; I am not afraid to go on the offensive in my approach to the demands and devastations that try to kill me from the outside-in.*

*I will stand, not as weak but as strong, knowing that You are in me, for me, and working out from me. I will not fear the destroyer but trust You, Who has made me an overcomer (Rom. 8:37). Amen.*

### 2. Let God Lead (Seek)

Give up and you'll land yourself in greater faith. Seek His moves, listen, and follow. Repeat.

### 3. Heed, Then Proceed

Like me, you may have days where you hate everything about yourself. You may have days where you say everything is far too gone, far too dead, and far too unsalvageable to be rescued. Pay heed to your feelings—wave hi and see them for what they are, then bring them before the throne and let them hang out with Jesus. He can hold them while you proceed, all systems go, to where He is leading you. Heed, then proceed.

Don't let who you were deter you, either.

Just think, adulterers are restored: Bathsheba, involved with a married man, got to carry the line of Jesus. Controllers are loved: Tamar, who faced being stoned for scandalous behavior, was restored to carry the lineage of Jesus. The bitter are made new: Naomi, who lost her family and seemingly all good things, was revived.

### 4. Don't Be Shocked If You Start to Bleed

Did you know "Jesus was led by the Spirit into the wilderness to be tempted by the devil" (Matt. 4:1)? The very hand of God led Jesus into a situation of evil, copious temptation, and a potential downfall. Why? Why would God allow this? Why would He bring us to horrible territory? I believe He brings us there to release us from the idea we won't or can't win. Our mini-victories against evil make us a stronger warrior in our fight for good.

Sometimes we have to learn "resist" before we can become God's great lobbyist. We have to go through enduring before we start conquering. We have to survive in the dark so we can thrive in the light.

Just think: it was in the wilderness where Jesus learned to walk in faithfulness—straight up to the cross.

If only we will see! What looks like a crying ground is often our training ground for God's transforming ground.

### 5. Expect to Be Freed

Where the Spirit of the Lord is, there is freedom (2 Cor. 3:17). Period. Expect it. Believe in it. Abide with God and He will lead you, to the day where you notice that, instead of your usual trudging, you are actually walking. You will see a new path emerge.

You notice you feel released from your heaviness. It feels like sparkles and rainbows and everything good. So you quicken your pace; you observe the rocks and take notice of every threat to your balance. And this time you don't waver and you don't back down; you step over the rocks and make your way around them. Even in those off times when you do lose your balance, you regain it, knowing that the journey is not about the absence of rocks but God's great power to lift you over them. You stick with God.

You run: to be more like Him.

You sprint: to be where He is.

You let go: shedding the weight that has kept you slow.

You anticipate: knowing the living water you are heading to consumes all suffering in the end.

You press on. Until there you stand, doused, drenched, and delivered. Until you find you are wading, looking straight up into His ever-pouring waterfall of love. And you remember her—you—the girl at the beach. The free one. The dancing one. The revived one. You don't worry so much about looming storms, or people, or sand whiplashing your eyes. No, you see the air, the tides, and the rocks as beautiful Presence instead of risky propositions. Peace settles. Daddy is with you. You grab His hand; you hear His voice of love. You trust Him and you feel *alive*. Rescued. Delivered.

New decrees settle within you:

> *If God is with me, then nothing can be against me (Rom. 8:31).*
>
> *If Spirit is in me, then God wants me.*
>
> *If Jesus is overcomer, then by His strength within me I can be too (Rom. 8:11).*

You grab His hand called *courage*, you look in His eyes, you feel the heat of His love and His voice of soothing water (Rev. 1:15)—and with full thanks and radiance you spin, round and round you go. Unencumbered. Unrestrained. Unbelievably whole with your Maker.

You have everything you could ever want—and more. You chose the right door.

## Something to Chew On

### Ten Things the Devil Wants You to Believe

1. You have to strive to thrive. *Truth: Jesus won and it is done.*

2. You have no identity; you must fill that fact with sin. *Truth: the Spirit testifies that you are a child of God.*

3. You aren't really forgiven. *Truth: your sin is farther from you than the east is from the west. It is cast into the farthest reaches of the ocean. It is never to be seen again.*

4. God has too much to do to guide someone like you. *Truth: God will always be with you. Nothing can ever separate you from the love of Christ Jesus.*

5. Sure, you know what God says, but with ever-available grace, you don't ever have to live it. *Truth: knowing God's love means living it. It's risky stuff for the devil.*

6. Make YOLO (you only live once) and FOMO (fear of missing out) your decrees. *Truth: living in the current moment with God means you are full of every single solitary thing that is astoundingly amazing. God-in-you is where the action is.*

7. Let feelings be your guide. *Truth: if you step away from letting the Holy Spirit be your guide, your feelings will be in charge and they will lead you down the road to doubt, discouragement, and despair (the devil's favorite landing pads).*

8. Live in your messy yesterday so you do no godly good today. *Truth: the only working place for life-change is right under our feet at this current hour.*

9. Live in fear. You will then know your good God is far from near. *Truth: we have not been given a*

*spirit of fear and timidity but of power, love, and a sound mind (2 Tim. 1:7).*

10. You may be saved for eternity but He won't help you today. *Truth: God is Redeemer. It is His name. He doesn't do it once but all the time. Believe, even with mustard seed–sized faith!*

Which of the above lies have you believed? If you are hearing accusations and condemnation, you can be sure they are not the voice of God. What have you felt accused of lately? Start to take a personal inventory of the accusations rendered against you and fight back with the Word of God.

*five*
# Control

## I Have to Have It

If I were to look back at my career, I think my greatest achievement is very simple. I've been able to make choices where I could glorify God.

Roma Downey

*I* try to be an I-can-figure-it-out-on-my-own type of girl—oh my goodness, I try. It is right about at this point when the Spirit pulls up and says, *All wisdom is Me. All change starts here.*

Okay! Got it now!

The only reason that I have even a grain-sized ability to speak about this whole issue is because the Spirit and I have been "conversating" about this—a lot. If you start fighting to be boss, God will do a lot of teaching about who really is. This is where we can learn something, I think. A lot, even.

If the Spirit goes about asking questions, giving directions, or replying with arrows sent directly, lightning-speed, to my heart, I have learned I'd better get listening.

If we get listening, we'll get growing—and maybe walk away with a little nugget of wisdom that was never ours to begin with, but because we serve a very good, good God, He gives it to us anyway.

## The Truth about Control

So here is my honest starting point. The one that proves I am far less an expert and far more just trying to grab His gold. My confession: my only strategy is to have a strategy.

It is to tell my little peons (aka my children) what to do.

It is to tell my come-to-my-rescue prince (aka my husband) how to improve things.

It is to tell my genie-in-a-bottle (aka God) He should give me what I want.

It is to tell my plebes (aka my friends) how to act.

It is to tell my war plan (aka my schedule) how to operate.

It is to tell others' feelings (aka my peace) how to be.

It is to tell my food (aka brownies, peanut butter, chocolate ice cream, and peanut butter cups) how to quell my emotions.

It is to tell my drink (aka Cabernet Sauvignon) to take my edge off.

It is to tell my life to fill my cup, my tummy, my household, my work, and my needs, and to guard me with panic room–like security. *Beep.* All secure.

But I am tired of faking strength. It isn't getting me anywhere and it keeps me locked in and unchanged.

God can more than handle a little control freak like me (and you). Here's the thing: it is not our abilities that make us able but rather His capabilities that make us more than able. It works like this: the Spirit of truth comes. He breaks through noise and speaks: *(Insert your name here), I know it all, and I am guiding you, (insert your name again), to all truth. I am speaking God's message that you must know, (insert your name here)* (John 16:13).

Our eyes open. We get wealthy when we realize real wealth is God. Seriously.

I know this is true. Why? Because when I control others by my treasured ideas, they rebel. Yet when God leads others by His truth, they land at peace. My terms don't really work out. His do.

With all this in mind, what I am seeing is that often our greatest act of faith is to allow the space in another's life for God to work. What might God do if you stepped down versus always trying to step in? If you prayed rather than trying to play savior?

No one is Creator except God. So why do we go about wrecking what He is likely re-creating?

Thanks, friends, for letting me vent. I feel like just acknowledging my dictator tendencies and my general proclivities somehow relieves me of the need to spout them out.

Exhale.

The words, "I don't know, God, but You do," are already helping me. The burden is not on me to write the story; I just have to let Him author so I can scribe. Then He will fill in the blanks that are bound to arise between all the lines in my mind.

He's faithful.

And He is already authoring an amazing story for you and me. Might you begin to believe in it?

## It's All about You

Just yesterday, my son validated the heart of my issue. He drew a picture of Mommy. I was curious, so I asked him, "What is Mommy doing in that picture?"

He said, "She is thinking."

He then drew the brain bubble that floats up in the sky like a hovering cloud of declaration. I said, "What is Mommy thinking about? What goes in that little bubble?" I was pretty certain I was just about to finally be crowned Super Mommy—the queen of peanut butter and jelly!

His answer? "She is thinking about herself."

Boom! And there you have it. With the force of a busted salt shaker hitting an open wound, I was stung with truth: Mommy is thinking about herself (again).

As controllers, it's hard not to be, isn't it?

We exchange relationship for rapid-fire orders.

We exchange love for lists.

We exchange being for doing.

We exchange journey for daily destinations, pickups, and deadlines.

We have the need to feel at ease, so we tend to forget other's deep needs.

Don't get me wrong; we have things handled. We are very good at reaching surface level, face value, and situational goals. That is covered. The floors are wiped and the Is are dotted and the Ts are crossed. But, just as my son revealed, sometimes we get so busy handling all we have to handle that we become dismantled. People suffer.

Deep breath. Exhale.

I know it is painful to admit. I feel it too.

Adventure, spontaneity, and curiosity—dead. Peace hindered. Joy lost. Tensions tightened. Ick! Yuck!

I don't want to live this way. I don't want to treat my children like little toy soldiers. I don't want my friends to feel like they live on my timeline. I don't want to find safety only inside the boundaries of my rigid lines. Those lines box me in to fear and it is now time to step outside that box.

## The Art of Not Knowing

It's right about this moment where a detailed woman, a try-harder like me, says, "I didn't do well, but I'll fix myself; I promise you. I will do whatever it takes to get things right. I'll drop and give you twenty, I'll find the answer online, or I'll make an action plan."

I. Will. Improve.

Personally, I'd do anything to make life okay; however, I am finding that usually all that needs to be said is this: "Lord!"

Not, "Lord! Those people should get their act together."

Not, "Lord! Things aren't going well, again?"

Not, "Lord! When will people move a little bit faster?"

Not, "Lord! If I want something done well, I have to do it myself."

Not, "Lord! I can't trust anyone."

Not, "Lord! When will You do what I need You to do?"

No, more like:

> *Lord! I need You, Jesus.*
> *Lord, I can't do it without You.*
> *Lord, saying I don't know how—it just scares me.*
> *That's why I need You. I am not sure what will happen when I let go. I just need You. I don't know how to fix people. I just need You. When I frantically try to fix and fashion things my way, I need You.*
> *Lord, help!*

It really just comes down to this: "Come, Lord! I don't want to be a dictator but rather an abider. Lord, I need You. I can't do it."

Did you notice that last statement? *I can't do it.*

Say it aloud. "I can't do it."

Scream it. "I can't do it!"

81

Yell it from a mountain, if you have to. "I. Can't. Do. It." You'll come alive.

## The "I Can't" God Uses as "Yes, You Can"

Look at this: "By faith we understand that the universe was formed at God's command" (Heb. 11:3). Does this hit you the way it does me?

God commands the seas. He commands the air we breathe. He commands the personalities of those around us. He commands the jobs we work at. He commands the steps in our day. He commands the things that come against us. He commands the rain that shows up on a wedding day and the clouds that part right before it. He commands it all.

If He is in command, how can we be?

It is equivalent to attending a business class at Harvard, making your way down to the front, moving the professor aside, and trying to explain the intricacies of US tax law—on your very first day.

"Move it, buddy. I have some thoughts on this!"

"The arrogance!" we would say in reply. Yes, I know, fellow courage-seekers—and this is me all the time.

"Get out of the way, Lord; I know how it should be done!"

All I have left to say is, "Sorry, God. Forgive me." And He does, friends. He does. And as I say, "Lord, help me," He runs to my rescue.

He does this for you too, you know?

Saying, "Lord, help me" has really worked and does work for those who trust His power. Consider the Israelites, who were wanderers at best and doubters at worst, but this time they trusted in the great help God would provide. Take a look: "It was by faith that the people of Israel went right through the Red Sea as though they were on dry ground" (Heb. 11:29 NLT).

It was not by work, it was not by planning, it was not by insight, it was not by intellect, it was not by advice-giving, it was not by power that the Israelites walked through a sea—it was by *faith*. Don't miss this point. You see, when you can't see because a sea of problems is blocking your view, it is your faith that will break up the torrents and currents.

Voyaging a little more, imagine standing right on the verge of your Promised Land, after nearly forty years of wandering, only to come face-to-face with an impenetrable wall. This would be the epitome of discouragement, right? It is like hearing the words, "Your breast cancer is in complete remission," only to then hear, "But we also found you have lung cancer." Disaster.

What?! What do you do when you can't force your dream to be reality? When you can't break the power of what stands before you? "It was by faith that the people of Israel marched around Jericho for seven days, and the walls came crashing down" (v. 30 NLT).

The Israelites marched circles around the city—not once but seven times on that seventh day, even though I am quite certain they probably felt like the village exercise and parade junkies. But still, they blew on rams' horns, they shouted loudly, and they kept going around and around.

I think they knew something we may not today: sometimes you have to keep on marching into what God has promised you, even when life wants to make a fool out of you. It's the moment you say, "Okay, God, I will do it Your way; even though to me it seems dumb and impossible and improbable." That is what God calls faith, which has nearly the same meaning as "landing at deliverance." What we have to come to terms with is that it doesn't always feel or look pretty.

When we get our arms wrapped around this fact, the walls start tumbling to the ground. Then faith has a party with all those who watched those walls crumble. What might God bring through you, if you trusted Him to really work through you—not by your power, posturing, or planning but solely by His?

Lord, help us!

### Letting Go, for Real

I know you. We in-charge types need a list—so here's the actionable version of "Lord, help me." Here's a how-to list for everyone like me—the ones who really want to know how to give it all up.

How to F.I.G.H.T. to let go:

*Forgo* the "blah, blah, blah" and fall into faith. Lean into the idea that when you release yourself from the role of commander, maker, and instructor, the Illuminator, the Holy Spirit, will guide you in the best way.

*Ignite* prayer. Simply say, "Lord, I believe; help my unbelief!" These six words have the power to change feelings, relationships, predicaments, and depression all in one fell swoop.

*Give* it up. Know there is no peace in maintaining another's peace.

*Help* yourself. Take a thousand-meter view of the problem. Look down on it and say, "Yes, there it is." Acknowledge it. Avoid judgment, criticism, and critique, and just see what God does with it.

*Treasure* God's truth as you carry these new decrees in your pocket:

*When I avoid my own conclusions, I often find God's.*

*Space and grace tend to lead to life and liberty.*

*A life in balance is found through a heart in prayer.*

When the Commander commands, the lover can lovingly follow. Let blind faith be your guide.

## Something to Chew On

**Awakening Courage:** Control, I hate you. I really do. You look like an offering of flowers but you smell like a bouquet of selfishness. You come to me with a smile and you leave those you touch with a frown. You fool me into thinking I can force love and then connive me into a hole of embarrassment. You suck me in with a charade of hope and make me think I can press square pegs into round holes, but it never works. You stink. You are the answer to everyone's problems that no one wants to hear. You are the excuse to those looking for an accomplice to the sin they are about to commit. You are the mirage we try to follow to change a person with no hope. You are the words *retaliation* and *manipulation* rolled into one. You spread your followers so thin they don't have any time left for God.

You make us assume responsibility for others' actions. You talk back to those who question you. You try to leave the once-alive dead in their trespasses. You know how to kill faith. You know how to stifle the oxygen of courage. You know how to beat down those who are trying. So, Control, you were not so good while you lasted—but today, be gone.

Today I won't listen to you but will instead listen to a new voice, mine, as I ask: *Am I handing out love or just demanding it?*

**Prayer Vase:** Start a prayer vase. Identify what you are prone to control each day. Rewrite each worry as a prayer on a small piece of paper and place it inside the vase, knowing what you forgo, He will grow. What you hand over will be handed back to you tenfold, greater than your wants and according to your heart's desires.

## *six*

# People Pleasing

### *You Will Like Me, No Matter What!*

After a while, you learn to ignore the names people call you
and just trust who you are.

*Shrek the Third*

Have you ever looked at your closet and decided that everything
in it needed to head to Salvation Army—about two years ago?
That is where I stood. I was looking at my closet, knowing I was
just about ready to meet with "those" women. I know you know
the type. They went to Ivy League schools, drive the perfect cars,
look stunning, and have the coveted handbag plus the shoes to
boot. Yep, these gals—they are called the whole package. They are
everything I fear I am not—and I had a feeling they would figure
it out in about a split second.

I looked at my reflection. It was the tired, worn, I-just-had-a-
baby reflection I'd expected. *How will they ever like me?*

I didn't know. I didn't know if all of this was even worth it.
Half of me wanted to meet with them; the other half of me just
wanted to stay home and hang out in exercise pants.

What do you do when your worst fear is that no matter how hard you try, or what you wear, or how you talk, you still won't be loved? Do you press in to what you know is about to take your insides and devour them, or do you run and run and run, outpacing those things that want to bother you?

I've run for a long time. Even while writing this book, right now, I am coming face-to-face with my running skills. I am like a runaway bride, if you will—but I guess it would be more accurate to call me a runaway friend.

I find faults with people before they find faults with me. I run.

If I write them off as not asking enough questions, I run. If I assume they're judging me, I run. If I find them boring, I run.

Running is far easier than staying to confirm they want to run from me first. So I guess I've found it easier to invest for a minute and then run for a lifetime. Sure, it gets tiring and lonely, but it is far better than the alternative, which is feeling like a reject once again.

I know some of those friends I've dissed are probably reading this book right now, and all I can say is—I am sorry I am a runaway friend. This chapter is my best effort to fix that, with God's help. But I digress.

As I stared at my reflection that day, pondering how to successfully show up with a gassy baby in tow *and* looking beautiful, a glimmer of hope surfaced. I saw it, like a shining star—the perfect blouse to do the job. Blue? White? Yes, it was perfect!

I could imagine me wearing it—and them receiving it. They would love my outfit. They would love my friendliness. They would love me. They would smile, run, and embrace the goodness of the moment upon my arrival, and hearts would fly as they laughed at my jokes, nodded at my stories, applauded my insights, asked me why they don't see me more often, and . . . there it stood, like a pimple on prom night. A gargantuan baby spit-up stain centered right across the right side of that perfect blouse. *Well, hello, I am*

*Kelly. It is so nice to meet you. I wear* eau de vomit *and you'll just love me. Give me a hug, I dare you.*

The longer I stared, the less able I was to hold the tears behind my strong-willed exterior. My hands shook. *What in the world do I have to offer? Why do I even bother?*

In the blink of an eye, I wasn't just the worst soon-to-be friend but also became the worst *everything.* I became an annoyance to all things good. The I-can't-do-anything-right woman. The no-one-will-ever-like-me lady. Everything seemed to stand up just to take me down. The laundry stood higher than the Empire State Building, the house was the messiest in the world, relational issues became monsters I would never tackle, and the dishes were going to break the back beneath the one shirt that couldn't even do its job—to make others like me. I was pathetic.

All I could think was, *Where are my exercise pants and the brownies I so intuitively stashed in the freezer?* Before too long, zebra stripes gave way to mascara puddles.

But then came clarity from my insanity: questions that made me reconsider everything.

*Is a friend a friend if she doesn't know the real me?*

*I mean, if she doesn't really know me, can she ever love me?*

*If all my joy is found in others' approval, can I really even count that as joy?*

*How can I be true to God if I can't be true to myself?*

We can become so covered with layers of "need to be liked," that, like onions, we have no conception of our core. Sometimes the cold shoulders, the disses, and the quick dismissals cut us—but in a good way. Sure, our stinging eyes tend to cry. Sure, we feel injured. The process hurts, I know, but joy is discovered when we get beyond the surface layers of what we think we want. It is when we get to the heart of what God wants for us that we find our own heart. It doesn't really matter so much, at that point, what others want. We become so peeled back by His refinement process that we get comfortable in our new skin.

We get comfortable when we begin to realize we are truly known. What smells odorous and odd about us, what we see as our worst traits—these stains, they aren't meant to be roughly rubbed away with a Tide stick. These things are meant to shine. They may be examples of all we believe we aren't but they are also promptings for us to see all who God is through them. He shows up for the meager ones, for the less-than. For me. For you.

At church yesterday, a girl was shocked when the pastor asked her to sing to thousands. She looked visibly shaken by the invitation, but she got up there and belted her heart out. I was touched, but all the same, the very moment she stepped up, all sheepish, I knew she would knock everyone's socks off. Why? Because God takes the weaklings, the ones who think they are bottom feeders, and nourishes His sheep.

We see our stains. God sees His glorious endgame. It works.

## Stained and Saved All the Same

What stain plagues you? What marks you as needing to be more than yourself? Needing to be a yes woman? Needing to have all the answers? Needing to appear just right?

Let me tell you something, child of God, and let me tell *me* something: even if everyone else is not pleased with you, God always is.

Did you know that?

Even when you are not true to yourself, even when you appease people, even when you are deathly afraid to speak your mind, your Father can't stop loving you. "But you were washed, you were sanctified, you were justified in the name of the Lord Jesus Christ and by the Spirit of our God" (1 Cor. 6:11).

He doesn't ridicule you; He doesn't get dominant or demanding; He doesn't tell you not to feel—or how to feel, for that matter.

He doesn't get turbulent, testy, or moody. He reaches out in love, calling you closer to His peace. He waits for you to turn toward His heart rather than trying to put on a song and dance routine for hearts that can never really love you enough.

Jesus Christ is ready to take your stain and make it into gain, if you let Him. Jesus died to wash you clean and now the Spirit is revealing all you need to walk a new walk. By His power, He'll wash you and send you off on a new path.

Will you let Him do His job?

There is nothing holding us back. There is no additional love we need to prove. There is no value we need to run after. There is no hope that isn't ours. There is no amount of proving and posturing that we need to uphold, for we are now holy, washed, recycled, and brand-new in Christ Jesus.

We no longer have to live wondering about what others think, for when God sees us sing and dance and play and move only for Him, He is well pleased.

With this truth, we can push other people to the exterior. Sure, we are called to love them, but we can stand and walk before our Maker unashamed, unabashed, and adored. We can look into His eyes and say, "May I please You?" And we can do it without feeling run over, taken advantage of, or lost. We can give Him our all and our best and more than last reserves. It is powerful.

When we assume this kind of posture the Spirit presses into us an understanding of our permanent new identity (2 Cor. 5:17). If we really listen with ears to hear and a will to receive and believe, we can begin to grab hold of the makings of who we truly are.

God is pleased with me (Gen. 1:31).

I am His masterpiece (Eph. 2:10).

I am a daughter, chosen until the end of ages (Gal. 4:7).

I am Jesus's friend (John 15:15).

I am raised up with Jesus and seated in the heavenly realms (Eph. 2:6–7).

I have fullness in Christ (Col. 2:10).

I may approach God with boldness, confidence, and freedom (Eph. 3:12).

The Lord will continually renew my strength (Isa. 40:29).

Christ is with me forevermore (Matt. 28:20).

I will one day be with Jesus in eternal glory (2 Tim. 2:10).

Instead of looking for false strength in the affections of others, remember you need the approval of only One. This makes all the difference, because when you see Christ Jesus is your backbone (Ps. 62:2), people no longer need to be.

It's as if you see them on the sidewalk but you also see that you are in the car with Jesus and you're heading to do the work He prepared for you in advance (Eph. 2:10). You have better places to be, so you don't worry so much. You start to consider bigger things, like, "What no eye has seen, what no ear has heard . . . [are] the things God has prepared for those who love him" (1 Cor. 2:9)

Now, if you are at all like me, then right about at this point you want to call me up and say, "Hey, Kelly, I know this stuff already. I have heard this a hundred and one times. Tell me something new."

And I would respond, "You don't need new. You just need to allow yourself to become renewed."

I know this because, probably like you, I start to think old things all the time. I get all caught up in the tracks and sound bites of yesterday in a way where I want high-fives and handshakes and cheers and accolades for what I have done. I want attention. But the Spirit whispers a different tune: "Put off your old self . . . to be made new in the attitude of your minds; and to put on the new self, created to be like God in true righteousness and holiness" (Eph. 4:22–24).

Perhaps you need to hear new again. I do too.

You press me further—which I love, by the way—"How, Kelly, how? How do we renew in a way that we can really start to think differently?"

I don't know. I don't have it all figured out. But what I do notice is that when I start making some little changes, something clicks.

## A View on How to Renew

1. **Face God.** This means to turn from everything that is not of God so that you can come face-to-face with everything that is of God. Paul defines this as "Repent and turn back" (see Acts 3:19). The Greek word *metanoeō* describes it as "to change your mind." What is the Spirit calling you to change your mind about (hint: ask)?

2. **Worship God.** You are called to behold God instead of humans. You are called to let the Spirit work renewal in a way where you get to sit in the presence of God and say, "Wow! You really are that great and You really do love me—holy cow!"

   Then, with an unstained and unveiled face, you may behold God's glory and be transformed to His image, by the work of the Lord who is the Spirit (2 Cor. 3:18).

3. **Pursue God.** When you put your mind in the center of the very place where the Spirit is living, active, and breathing (Heb. 4:12), you should expect to be changed. I guess that is why God calls His Word the Sword of the Spirit; it slices and dices all the sickly parts right out of us.

In the end, though, friends, what it comes down to is this: we can't lose heart (2 Cor. 4:16). I think God writes this because some days we are going to feel like a pile of dog poo. Some days we are going to feel like the things of old are about to tackle us. Expect this kind of thing, Paul tells us, and don't lose heart. He goes on to say, "Though outwardly we are wasting away, yet inwardly we are being renewed day by day" (2 Cor. 4:16).

I take this to mean: *You are going to mess up; you are going to start getting consumed with those people and their problems, and making them love you and saying yes all the time and forgetting about what I am doing in you, but remember this, dear child, child of My very own blood: I am still renewing you.*

I hear all this. I also hear decrees like:

> *Your stain is really your gain.*
>
> *When God really sees, who cares if others don't?*
>
> *Eyes set on God see little earth-shifting earthquakes that blind folk don't notice.*

God calls, ready to move us . . . ready to lead us to *new*.

From affirmation leech to embracer of truthful speech.

From pressure-laden to peace-filled.

From have-to to get-to.

From the idolatry of our "ideal" to the identity of His "real."

From indecision to decision in the Spirit.

From self-consumed to God-consumed.

From "needed" by others to equipped by God.

From exhausted to renewed.

From "rescuer" to needing rescue.

From being liked by others to being loved by God.

From giving to receiving.

From striving to abiding.

Will you answer His call? Will you let the plates of your foundation shift to see His wild affection for you?

It becomes a little secret—one between you and God. Or maybe you prefer to think of it as an inside joke. Because when you look in the mirror with that stained shirt on, your eyes see past it and what reflects back instead is the image of Christ (2 Cor. 3:18). You laugh. Not because it is tremendously funny but because it is wholeheartedly astonishing. And you cry too, not because you are cutting an onion or anything but because you really, truly feel loved as you have never been before. You get a sense that you have all you need—and you finally see that, in Him, it is more than enough.

What happened with me and that shirt? I left the house feeling stained, renewed, and quite certain that God was going to use it for some amazing discussion.

## *Something to Chew On*

**Awakening a Child of Calm:** Place these words on your mirror, nightstand, office desk, or on the back of your hand; I don't care, just hold on to this like a winning lottery ticket.

*My love, every amazing gift is from Me. I give much (James 1:17). I can't help but cherish you wildly and forever (Jer. 31:3). What you may not know is My perfect love casts out fear—not once but all the time (1 John 4:18); it is always working for you. In this way, you don't have a spirit of fear but of power, love, and self-discipline (2 Tim. 1:7). Did you know? You are wonderfully made (Ps. 139:14). I declare you as Mine; I take care of My children, whom I love (1 John 3:1). I rejoice over you; I can't stop thinking of you (Exod. 19:5, Zeph. 3:17; Ps. 139:3). I supersede opinions, perceptions, and reactions. I am the great I AM who covers over your words of "I am not" with "you can." Don't forget that I am for you, not against you (Rom. 8:31). I have set you free and free you are (John 8:36). I have not come to punish you (John 3:17), for My ways are better than* your best conceived plans (Isa. 55:8). *What you need to remember is I am the King of second chances; this is how I reign (1 John 1:9), and I will love you every time, no matter what anyone else does or says (Ps. 100:5). I am every good expression of love (Ps. 108:4). What I have bound together, no one can separate (Mark 10:9). The cross cannot be undone (Ps. 33:11). This means your sins are thrown from you as far as the east is from the west (Ps. 103:12). I have no condemnation left for you (Rom. 8:1). Will you trust Me? Will you let Me lead you? I promise not to leave you or forget about you (Deut. 31:8).*

### A Prayer for Stress Reduction

*God, who is the Spirit, I haven't known You. But maybe I should have. I want to open the eyes of my heart to see You and the ears of my willingness to hear You—so I can know You. May I come ready, not as one with defined parameters of Your work but one with open barriers and no limits for how far Your work may extend. Don't let me sit in stagnant old waters but push the boundaries of Your love so that my heart can't help but enter the rushing waters that are You. You are where life-change flows. Amen.*

## *seven*
# Worry

*If You Can't Beat It, Worry about It*

Being out there in the ocean, God's creation, it's like a gift He has given us to enjoy.

Bethany Hamilton, professional surfer

*I*'ve hung out with worry a lot. If I named a best friend it would probably be him. We get along really well—until I come to hate him and then want to kill him. Part of the problem is that we know each other too intimately; really, we've grown up together. And once you know someone so well, it can be hard to banish them—even if you know they aren't good for you. I guess he's like the good drug that I know is bad. I am not sure where else to turn to make things better, so I kind of fall back to him, thinking that in some shape, way, or form, together we will find our way.

We never do. He always leaves me cold, shivering, and feeling that pit in my stomach.

What about you?

Back in elementary school, I wouldn't have been called the sharp one. My homework papers were the ones filled with smudged eraser marks and tears. My mission at school was to count down the hours, first to lunch and then to recess and then to the end of the day. When the going got tough, I normally faked like someone had gotten rough and then found reprieve in the nurse's office. Safety!

Yet some days, despite my best efforts, I would end up stuck— with no get-out-of-class-free card. One such day, a day I couldn't escape, I was waiting to get my test from the previous week back. I knew what was coming but still wished that some divine intervention had happened and, somehow, I had blindly circled all the right choices. No luck. My teacher slammed it onto my desk: a big fat F.

My heart thumped in my chest, my hands got clammy, and my feet moved incessantly; I was in trouble with this one. The room nearly closed in on me when the teacher said, "I want this test signed by your parents and returned tomorrow."

Signed!? I knew I would have to pay. I could envision the punishments and the tears and the slamming doors. The looming, loud voices and lectures and the aggravation already sat heavy over me. For an instant, it seemed as if the whole class turned in unison to give me a dirty look. *I know, you all. I stink.*

I went home but at least had the intelligence to put the test paper in my pocket. Can't have Mom fishing around in my book bag. Must consider all the "options." Must avoid pain at all costs.

And so I carefully forged my mom's name on my paper of failure. Worry and me, we had a plan. We could figure things out together. We would forge our own destiny.

And we did. Mission accomplished. For a moment things felt kind of good.

Worry makes you imagine a great fight while you sit around and do mostly nothing to accomplish anything. Because, well, you know. You *know*. With worry, all you do is wrestle yourself—and get nowhere. It's a losing game right from the start. The only thing worry succeeds in producing in my life is a whole lot of agony.

The next moment all I could do was stare at what I had done. There was no erasing my forgery. It not only reflected the fact that I had tricked her but also that I, once again, was the bad child. Why was I so dumb?

The permanent marker couldn't erase my feelings nor the injury I was now forced to commit. I felt stuck with nowhere left to go. The more I glared at it, the more I couldn't stop thinking, *I can't wipe away the fact that I keep getting dumber and dumber.*

Worry convicts. It will not only knock out your mind but also sweep your whole identity from you in one fell swoop. It will get you saying (and believing):

This marriage will never work.

My child will never love me.

I will never beat my past.

I will always be in financial ruin.

I am a mess.

I am powerless.

I am a victim.

God is angry at me. He is going to get out His belt and I am going to really get it for this one. No one helps a child as repetitively bad as me. He will have to really teach me a lesson on this one.

What does worry often whisper in your ear—about yourself and about how God sees you?

I was hearing: *You always make messes. You will never be smart. Figure out something to do about it.*

Let me mention that this was not the first time this kind of thing had happened to me. But last time, worry and I, well, we handled it another way. We went into my neighbor's yard, dug a hole, and buried my test under their bush for safekeeping. Problem solved.

"The dog ate my homework" wasn't a lie for once. I was proud—kind of.

I got away with it then, but this particular time, when I took my forgery to class, I ended up in the principal's office, Mexican-standoff style. It was me versus her and all I can say is that I really didn't want to fold, but she said she was going to call my parents and there were no other avenues worry and I could go. So we gave in. We then became stuck in a huge hole of *consequences*. I got really mad at worry over that one, I assure you.

This is how it is with worry, isn't it? He convinces you that you can make a way, when all along the only way is—and always was—Jesus (John 14:6). Sometimes we have to go the wrong way to realize it.

All this to say that I want to break up with worry; he is a horrible friend.

## What Dwells

My parents always seemed to make this point to me when I was a kid: you become like the company you keep. They normally mentioned it as I was about to go to *that* girl's house. Looking back, I see the truth in this line of thinking. What you dwell around will before long dwell in you.

What do you dwell around? Catastrophic news? Negative friends? Never-ending political ranting? Compromising temptations? Worry? Anxiety?

Worry is like gossip. It is continual talk and all bad feelings. Endless chatter and no progress. Tons of opinion and no love. It's like a never-ending game of telephone that moves relationships nowhere. Round and round it goes—talking about a whole bunch of garbage that never brings progress. Still, we women—we rely on it like a best friend, don't we? We think it will get us ahead, maybe prevent us from being third-tier, marginal, or left behind. That's how we figure it, anyway. *Better get figuring, because God is out there doing nothing. He's being silent again and His silence means that I have to step up and figure things out myself!*

The beliefs that live in our mind will pour out through our actions. What lives in your mind? Christ or worry? Faithfulness or abandonment?

The scary part is, if worry dwells there, then apprehension, anguish, and anxiety will only release anger, apathy, and aggravation. Yuck. Our soul then tells our body what to do and we respond with a whole host of medical issues, including paranoia, stress disorders, drug and alcohol abuse, insomnia, eating disorders, and more.[1]

So, what is the solution?

> Finally, brothers and sisters, whatever is true, whatever is noble, whatever is right, whatever is pure, whatever is lovely, whatever is admirable—if anything is excellent or praiseworthy—think about such things. (Phil. 4:8)

I think Paul had good intentions here with this verse, I really do, but putting it into practice is another story. Living this out? It's hard. When I try to back up and see why it is so hard, it comes down to something like this: What if I think good things but only get left with bad?

How do I push forward with God after that?

Worry, though, seems to work for me, to help me in some odd way, almost like an insurance policy that pays off in the long term so I don't have to feel let down by God. It feels like: *At least I know my loss is my fault.* I don't have to worry about finding out God isn't so good after all.

But the truth is, I am getting tired. I am getting beaten. I don't want to live life as a wreck; I want to live as a worshiper and a warrior, not a worrier. Frankly, worry is a bad coach; he is the opponent to everything I want.

I have the power to demote him, and so do you. What do you say we kick him out of our ring?

## A Good Hangout

It all comes back to what you dwell around.

> Whoever dwells in the shelter of the Most High
>     will rest in the shadow of the Almighty.
> I will say of the LORD, 'He is my refuge and my fortress,
>     my God, in whom I trust. . . .
> No harm will overtake you, no disaster will come near
>     your tent. (Ps. 91:1–2, 10)

Here's our hope:

1. Dwelling with God provides shelter. (*Stopping* to see where God is.)
2. Staying under that shelter keeps us dry and safe. (*Dropping* under His cover.)
3. By trusting Him we know we will make it. (*Rolling* ahead by faith.)

Now, let's take a moment: Did you notice, in the verses above, what we find in shelter? Did you see it too? It's that one thing that always seems to elude every woman I know. It is *rest*. Imagine that! I'll take it!

Even more, when I look at these three things, what overwhelms me is this: I want to live this way. I want to *stop* when the world crashes in, I want to *drop* into His sheltered place when I feel unsteady, and I want to *roll* into purpose when circumstances start pushing me.

I want to stop, drop, and roll. Do you?

It is our way to escape. Sometimes the best way to fight is to turn and run to God's lands of peace.

Sometimes we feel like we are doing nothing. We feel like we are stagnant in seeking and praying and longing for God, but we aren't. When we dwell in the shadow of our all-loving Lord, He covers us in the protection of His all-consuming safety. Progress!

It is in this dwelling place—in His love, in His Word, in His being, in His favor, in His vision, and in His future for us—that we find peace. This means we don't need strategies and tricks and schemes; we just need sheltered thoughts and beliefs.

We simply stop to see, drop to our knees, and roll on with His protection over us, until the day He reveals to us that we are now different—full of character, endurance, perseverance, and greater faith.

Worry doesn't work for us. God does.

Open His invitation. The Spirit calls us to a greater dwelling place—a place where longings are fulfilled, where God-stuff happens, where truth shines, and where lives get put back together into a mosaic of more.

"You'll become like the company you keep!" If we keep the company of the Spirit, like whom will we become?

### Spirit Dwelling

I am convinced that to worry is to listen to the voice of the flesh that says, *You are about to die.* But the Holy Spirit is about us listening to the voice of God that says, *In My realm you are about to find life—and live it big* (John 6:63; 10:10; Rom. 8:9). It means: here is goodness, pureness, rightness, and peace. I'll just grab me some of that.

It all comes down to staying in tandem with the Spirit. To be led by Him continually. It works, you see, because the Spirit is antiworry by His nature, and He dwells within our body, which is all flesh (continually self-motivated). We are either driven one way or the other, just as selfless is the opposite of selfish—we can't simultaneously be both.

I know you all know how it works—we either think *faith* or we think *fear*. They can't coexist. See what I mean?

In this I can't help but feel a little tug on my heart that says, *Right here, Kelly; this click of clarity makes all the difference.*

I want to figure this thing out, I really do, but usually I hardly give thought to flesh versus Spirit. It's not like I wake up in the morning saying, "Oh, flesh, take a hike, you're leading me wrong," or, "Hey, Spirit, I want to find Your life."

We just don't tend to think this way; I certainly don't think this way. I tend to think much more about kids being late to school, car problems, rain ruining my weekend plans, and annoyances with others than I do about the power of God as I dwell with Him—and I don't know, but maybe this is my real problem.

Because when it comes down to it, isn't life just made up of a bunch of choices? Ones where we must decide if we will abide by our flesh (our desires, cravings, and demands) or by the Spirit? Where we choose to live by either our outer voice of ruin or God's inner voice of peace?

If you love one, you normally turn away from the other.

You see, worry fills us one way and the Spirit fills us another. Worry usually leads us to a way of regret and the Spirit leads us to "the Way" (aka Jesus). Worry dwells all around us, making unreal catastrophes seem so real, and the indwelling Spirit settles our mind on a path called "Wow!" There is no middle ground. You either dwell in one place or the other. You either see potential life or looming death.

I can almost hear you all coming after me, ready to say, "Now, Kelly, fear friend, this sounds all fine and dandy, but what does it even mean to be filled with the Spirit? Explain!"

To answer your question, it is first crucial to know who the Spirit is, so we can know what He does.

### 1. The Spirit Empowers

The "power of the Spirit" propelled the gospel far and wide (Rom. 15:19), directed Jesus where to go (Luke 4:14), and strengthens us in power (Eph. 3:16). If the Spirit could compel Jesus's movements, don't you think He has the power to positively direct ours?

### 2. The Spirit Leads

"Those who are led by the Spirit of God are the children of God" (Rom. 8:14). Is there any way that the most incredible, capable, powerful, and loving Daddy would abandon you, the very child He sent His one and only Son to save (John 3:16)? If God didn't waste His time caring for you on the cross, I can assure you He's not wasting His time leading you today.

### 3. The Spirit Fills

"Be filled with the Spirit" (Eph. 5:18). The Spirit doesn't want a portion of your mind; He wants all of it, so He can pour out His good things. When you dwell in the fullness of God, you live in the greatness of His love.

Clear room for the Spirit to fill you, and guess what? He will.

The problem is, I usually don't. I tend to leave junk heaped all over the place. Frankly, I make God's temple look like a mess. What pains me even more about the fact that I tend to clutter God's vital dwelling space is that this kind of approach actually causes grief to Him too (4:30).

Oh, man.

I hate being the one who has caused the Spirit grief, don't you? In a way, I kind of want to pause from writing, set down this book, and give myself a silent talking to, except for one thing: God cares far more about where we are going with Him than He does about things He's already forgiven. Have you asked Him to forgive you for the grief you've intentionally or unintentionally caused?

Let's clean up our junk. The temple was made to be holy and, as we women know, sometimes we have to go in and do a deep clean before the guest arrives. Get out your dusters, ladies; we're going to welcome the Spirit with an even greater sparkle.

How do we do it? How do we welcome the indwelling Spirit, the most VIP of VIP guests? Here's how warm W.E.L.C.O.M.E. works:

*Wait*. God did not press the pause button to keep you frozen in horrible circumstances. He's working things out so He can arrive with unfathomable insights and perspective.

*Experience*. Look left, look right, look up, look down. Find His displays of love through nature, the little things, the big things, uplifting songs, and praise. They are His housewarming gifts to you.

*Let* the truth be told. Rather than trying to be like Eve, who hid and blamed, let God see where you stand. Say, "Yes, it is me. I failed again. Will You forgive me? I want all of You." He turns toward hearts that turn toward Him.

*Come* back to prayer, again and again. The second you feel disconnected, get reconnected with the faith that can move mountains (Matt. 17:20).

*Open* the Bible. Let in truth. Your long-held fleshly perspectives on your long term are certain to get uncomfortable when Christ's love settles in.

*Meditate* and communicate. Sit down with God's Word. Close your eyes. Envision yourself in the story. Ask to be led, guided, and filled. Let the Spirit direct the course of His entire visit.

*Eyes* attentive. Keep your eyes on the One with you. Don't get distracted; your first Love is right with you, in the center of your very home. Enjoy Him with your full presence.

Will we welcome? Will we choose to stop, drop, and roll out a red carpet for the Spirit, or will we continue to worry and say, "Nope. Not enough space here for You"?

The answer often determines if we find peace with God or panic with our old, hated friend, worry.

When it comes down to it, our dwelling capacity has so much to do with our future destiny. I want to make room for all things Spirit so badly. What about you? Let's become like the company we keep.

## When Empowering, Leading, and Filling Take Root

He searches the earth. He looks far and He looks wide. He looks at you and He looks at me; His eyes seek and home in on committed hearts, on the steadfast folk (2 Chron. 16:9). Do His eyes land on us?

Does He find us sowing not from the flesh but to please the Spirit (Gal. 6:8)? Or are we simply wrestlers with life, pursuers of self, and gainers of all things worldly?

May we be the ones God searches for. Oh, what a dream that would be—that He would find us, the fear fighters, standing and looking back at Him. There we would be; I can almost see it. I see us grabbing hands, circling this terror-laden and nearly explosive world as a tight-knit band, a force to be reckoned with, pulling together in His name. The power! He used to know us as the fearful ones, but no more. Now we are the faithful ones. Not because we do things right or perfectly all the time but because we are now allowing Him to make things right within us. We are accepting Him, we are submitted, we are calling, and we are looking for Him like never before.

God sees that kind of thing, I reckon.

We don't have to figure and fact check; we just fall on our knees. We don't have to be Bible-Britannicas; we solely need our new mindset of holy, right, and pure. We don't have to have a Bible verse for every worry that surfaces; we just have to stop, drop, and roll. I am pretty certain we don't even have to stand there as ones who "always feel great" but rather as ones who never give up the fight.

I always had to fight in school. I had to fight to figure out left and right. I had to fight to learn to read. I had to fight to try to not stay back in third grade (I lost). I had to fight to not seem dumb. I worked hard. So hard. Extra hard. In many ways it was all worth it, because in my fight I learned how to not give up, not back down, and not think that everything would come easy.

And what I see today is that fighting is not so much about doing religion—or trying or striving or thriving—as much as it is about doing every single, solitary thing to ensure that the love of Jesus and the power of the Spirit have first rights to your heart over your flesh. Then selflessness can step out to hand out what has been so graciously distributed to you, a poor old soul.

That is the fight.

This repentance, release, and renewal process, when we are open to it, is us fighting the good fight. Are you fighting it? It pulverizes worry and demolishes those deplorable agreements the devil loves to wave over our heads. It sounds a whole lot like this:

*To You, God, may we return. Spirit, we incline our heart to You. Keep us in safety. Expand us in faith. Diminish our fear. Give us Your everything. We will seek your face. Your face we will seek (Ps. 27:8). We'll bow low like a lamb but fight for You like a lion—knowing that when we seek You, we will find You (Jer. 29:13). We will expect this. We will wait for this. We will be certain that You have us in the palm of Your hand and that no depletion of bank accounts or winds of destruction can make us fall. We will know. And as we know You more, we will know we're united, as two kindred friends (John 15:15) who need nothing but each other.*

Fullness.

Satisfaction.

Freedom evermore.

Release.

We don't always have to come strong—because He is the one with the brute strength (2 Cor. 12:9).

We seize what He offers us, what we feel. We seize it because we are certain we have found something that counts. It is called faith; it hardly leaves room for fear. It takes a weak one and makes her strong. It confounds the wise. It brings the spiritual realm to life. It makes the poor rich. It helps the blind see. It returns the dead to life. It gives steadfast hope to those who suffer. It cares far less about circumstances and far more about eternal survival. It takes each "I can't" and turns it into "I can." It is the window to God's heart that leaves no room for worry, for that kind of nature can't be seen from this vantage point. And, without a doubt, we can know, more than anything we have ever done or postured to do, that *this counts.*

Maybe it counts more than anything else we have ever done. New decrees rise:

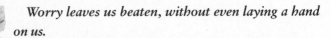

*Worry leaves us beaten, without even laying a hand on us.*

*Where the Spirit is—there is freedom (2 Cor. 3:17).*

*It is by dwelling with the Spirit that we go about abiding in the Lord.*

*Worry only works if we take our eyes off God.*

We grab on to our hidden weapon: Spirit. We run, we stop, we drop on the mat, and we roll in some fantastic way we never believed we could before. And when we stand up, it is not the gymnastics fans who applaud our great moves, it is God. He says, *Your brilliance is Me. I flip things over in the blink of an eye; I give eternal hope that worry can't steal and I do exceedingly, abundantly more than you can ask or imagine (Eph. 3:20). Will you continue to trust Me?*

## Something to Chew On

### Seven Practical Life Tips to Find Calm

1. Wake up in praise. Before you think, *How do I press snooze?* speak praise. Declare, "God, You are good. I will trust You today. I give my all to You."
2. Be still. Quiet your mind. Quiet your soul. Sit. Listen. Ask God to speak to you. Then picture Jesus. Hear His heart to you. Listen for His words over you (reminder: accusation is not from God).
3. Inhale calm. Exhale body tightness. Inhale peace. Exhale things not of God. Inhale forgiveness. Exhale guilt. Inhale love. Exhale fear. Inhale purpose. Exhale lies. Inhale. Exhale. Pray, and give thanks.
4. Call a friend who listens. Tell her it is time to let you vent. Then do so. Bonus: ask her to pray (yes, in that very moment). Then pray for her.
5. Serve someone in need. Go do it. See how you feel after.
6. Forgive yourself or someone else. Let it go. Again, see how you feel after.
7. Worship. Turn on music that reminds you of who you are in Christ. Let these tunes transform your insides.

# *eight*
# Comparison and Competition

## *As Long As I Am Better Than You . . .*

Always be a first-rate version of yourself, instead of a second-rate version of somebody else.

Judy Garland

*Once upon a time . . .* Free Spirit was free. She danced to the wind of truth and moved to the beat of life. She knew her tribe, her clan, and her origin. Spirit, vision, and fire pulsed within her; they made her beautiful, vibrant, and untethered. She loved to sway, heart-to-heart, beating as one with her Chief. She lived in the freedom of the wild, the calling of the One, with the movement of His wind at her back. She knew peace was found camped right in the center of His love. She didn't need much else. Her face was painted with joy.

Yet one day, as happens with so many resolute ones, Free Spirit's eyes darted to things not native—things dashing before her. And then she saw them—Shifting Shadows, nearly indiscernible but captivating all the same. She stepped toward them.

Wow. Their somewhat hazy confidence was staggering. It was something. And in that moment she knew their *something* was the *everything* she didn't have.

And after watching these tall and beautiful Shifting Shadows all day, nearly every day, Free Spirit realized other things. She wasn't living blessings, she was entirely failing. More than that, her Chief wasn't giving her good stuff; He only gave average. His names for her didn't mean much; His promises seemed worthless. She was bored of her childlike attitude. She didn't much care to ask for help. She didn't much care to wait around for promises and supposed great-things-to-come. She didn't much care what her Chief said about her or what He had done for her in the past. She wanted a more sophisticated life now. She would be smart, skinny, and super like those other girls, the Shifting Shadows.

She ran away from her tribe.

Free Spirit knew if she could make it there, on her own, she could make it anywhere. And she would. To her, abiding was cliché and loving was so last year—but striving, she surmised, was her golden ticket.

Whispering to the Shifting Shadows, she made a quiet oath, *I will follow you.*

Her Chief watched her from a distance. His heart broke because He knew His vision—His uniquely tailored plans made just for her. He didn't want to see her exchange His best for their average. He lamented how she believed in her weakness instead of His ever-flowing strength. He had grown, nurtured, and pressed endurance in her with such care and precision, and now, to see her pass it all off for second-rate appearances—it pained Him. The distance between the Chief and Free Spirit was palpable. He longed with a jealous love for the one who once danced with Him. Maybe, just maybe, she would come to believe in what He already knew to be true about her.

He watched her move her hands left and right, trying to grab hold of the Shifting Shadows but, like a blindfolded toddler, all she grabbed was nothing, dead air. She grew frustrated and exasperated.

Huffing and puffing, she stripped off her tribal colors, removed her warrior gear, changed her attitude, and grayed her appearance. She stood looking nothing like the Chief's image anymore (2 Cor. 3:18).

Free Spirit lost her conception of the Holy Spirit. The Chief became grieved.

She felt more foreigner than native, more runaway than belonging, and more poor than rich. She needed something to take the edge off; nothing sufficed. She needed a shopping thrill, but it didn't do the trick.

She knew her name was no longer Free Spirit but Captured Misfit.

Her Chief didn't see her this way though. He drew up a large swell of wind and blew it against her back. He hoped she would remember who she was and where she came from.

And this time, she did.

Eyes opened, she saw. At the top of the hill, He was waiting with loving eyes and a warm smile. Her Daddy, her Chief: mighty, strong, and smiling. She fell to the ground and cried. He met her there. She finally knew her way out.

She stood tall, grabbed her warrior gear, and ran with newfound courage straight up to the Shifting Shadows. She wanted to expose the truth. And she found it as she hit them with her light—there simply was nothing there. They were not real.

Finally, she understood: this whole time, what she chased and what drove her mad was her very own fear that she was not good enough for the identity so freely given by a Chief like Him. It was never about beauty or success or looks or clothes or kids; it was all about believing in herself as He saw her. She felt so exhilarated, so stupefied. She didn't know how to handle it.

She looked at those shadows and screamed.

She screamed, "I am who He says I am! No one can ever take that from me!"

And she walked on home.

## The Rosie Story

Rosie. This girl has every reason to chase shifting shadows. Why? Because from the vantage point of the world, there's so much her hands can't do.

Rosie, by all accounts, has a lot to make up for. She has a lot to prove. She has a lot of work to do to make you like her. She's "half armed" in this world. Not in the spiritual sense, because this woman is completely armed in prayer, but I am talking about an entirely different way.

She is literally half-armed.

With two stubs and two dangling fingers, she is the kind of person you glance at but don't really look at. She is the kind you steer clear of because you fear your three-year-old will inadvertently ask *that* question. She is the kind who makes you nervous because you fear she'll know how nervous you really are. Can't get caught!

I know you'd feel all this, because it's pretty much what everyone feels when they meet her.

Some might look at Rosie and say, "Why didn't she shut down shop and get depressed long ago?" And I don't know; maybe she's asked herself these same types of questions too. Questions like, *Why am I the one stuck living manicure-free my whole life while everyone else has color? Why can't I drive, like that girl? Why do I have difficulty? Why did God make me this way?*

If deficiency becomes your identity, there's no doubt you'll walk with a defeatist mentality. You'll either try to make up for all that you're not or abandon all that you are—and never leave your house.

Rosie chose the former. Unable to drive to meet her friends, she called up a cab and grabbed her young son. She didn't want to be a burden and ask for help. She didn't want to be a nuisance. After all, she had to stand tall with the cool girls—this meant not allowing a drop of sweat to fall. This meant appearing super strong, in a way where she more than made up for anything they might have thought she lacked. Confidence must rule. And there was no way she would let her guard down. Certainly not! That would prove her weakness, highlight her inferiority, and drive home the nagging feeling of not belonging.

She could not have that.

She could do it and would do it—well—on her own. She would go the extra mile to be the best mom ever, the best friend ever, the best woman ever, and the best at getting herself anywhere without the help of anyone.

She went outside to wait for the cab, toddler in tow. It didn't help that the temperature was well below freezing. It didn't help that hail was pummeling her and her boy. She just shivered and stood tall and waited for the driver to pick her up. Fifteen minutes passed. Twenty minutes. Forty-five minutes. Her little one froze. And as they waited, Rosie couldn't help remembering all she had kept doing in order to be more than enough: the constant babysitting, the meals, and everything else she did to go the extra mile for her friends. But what if all her efforts were worthless? What if they still thought, *She's not like us*?

Her toes were beginning to feel numb from being outside too long and her heart was starting to feel the same, from outdoing herself. She glanced at her son; he was red-faced too. She nudged him a bit and said, "Let's go!" She pushed that kid down the ice-laden road, looking left and right for the taxi, hating every minute of it.

Every step seemed to confirm all she wasn't. *My silhouette? It's not like theirs. My personality? Is it even a match?* This game of trying and pining to win, to be more, and to rise above her own inadequacy was just leaving her tired.

Overcompensating is exhausting! Do you size people up and then supersize yourself to make sure you're not a misfit?

I do. I either think I am the worst or I think I am the best. It is a pendulum of pride—a winning or losing game that never stops to land at calm. Back and forth, back and forth it goes—the constant momentum of uncertainty that you'll be okay, accepted, or acknowledged in this world.

It's the show that never ends. We put on our costume and we overdo our makeup and we head out, thinking that all that show will distract others from who we really are—except for one thing: it never does. God sees through it all. He already sees the real me.

But God doesn't hate the likes of Rosie and me, those who go about trying to be more than He made us to be—so we can feel better than our reality called "me." He doesn't disregard, demean, or denounce us, based on our "bad attitudes." He doesn't laugh at us behind our backs. Nope. He doesn't send us to bed with no dinner, He doesn't sigh over us with exasperation, and He doesn't zap us from heaven by the power of an iron-fisted hand.

He calls us. He calls us to come, so the Spirit can push revealing and heart-warming truth right up against us.

And we do come. We grab the truth, because not looking at Him means we have to keep on struggling. We kind of feel over that. We feel like God has more for us in this busted-up garden called life than just living with a bouquet of wilted weeds that only represent our "failures."

We want to grab hold of His *more*.

So, as we cuddle in next to Truth, we reach deep and what we pull out is our own personal trinket, displaying what each of us had been missing for a long, long time. We pull it out and we see that because we had been looking at everyone else, we've missed looking at Him. We realize, when we hold this little trinket of our being, made perfectly by His being, He could possibly use us just as we are—faulted, mangled, and jacked-up in our own right.

For it is the humble ones, the malleable ones, that God most shapes for His great purposes.

We want to be that kind of woman. The kind of woman who shines brightly and brilliantly, unafraid of the image of Jesus in her. Even more, we want to be free to let it all loose, even if it looks untamed, uncontained, or unashamed.

For you're not really *you* until you follow the lead of Christ in you.

Then it hits us even more. It comes down to a choice: we will either spend our lives making ourselves "more" or we will abandon ourselves to find God's more. If we see ourselves as His beloved, if we see His truth written all over our genetic makeup, if we see His purposes, what begins to grow inside us is a seed called *passion*. No longer will weeds called demotivation and discouragement pop up. No longer will they grow and bunch together in a haphazard bouquet. Instead, we will see ourselves in a glory-filled garden intended to display the wonder and beauty of God. We will sway with His wind.

The garden is a place of abundance, joy, and peace.

Rosie came in from the cold and listened for God's voice. And God met her there, telling her, *Don't look at what you have to do or what others want you to do; just follow what I've called you to do.*

When we step outside perfect, poised, and powerful, we hear the quiet voice of God calling us to discover what we never knew we hoped for.

For Rosie, prayer ensued, comparing faded, and vision surfaced. She found a "meeting place" with God. It is in these types of meeting places that measurers and stacker-uppers, wannabes and beauty queens, settle down to plead and pray, to pine and ponder all things God. In this place, we almost can't help but cross paths with Him—and with mission.

It is where we let go.

It is where God speaks the unimaginable.

It is where competing women unwind and delight and commit to God's ways. And, in turn, God gives us the unsaid desires of our heart (Ps. 37:4–5).

It's where new thoughts and decrees become cemented, words like:

> *When we set aside competition we find connection—with God and others.*
>
> *When we abandon comparison we hit mission.*
>
> *What we see as our hindrance, God sees as admittance to behold His radiance.*

Rosie stood on a cliff of great opportunity with no idea how or why or where God would take her. She had no clue if people would pity her rather than ponder her great art. She was uncertain if people might consider her a freak show instead of a respected show.

But it didn't matter. And it doesn't matter.

You see, if God wants you to do it, He will part the Red Sea to bring you to it. You just have to move in—even though fear is trying to get you to back out. That is what Rosie did.

She simply closed her eyes, mustered her courage, and moved—and by faith, despite fear, she painted. Not with her hands but with her feet. Not feeling half-equipped but fully equipped. Not feeling less than whole but rather a radiant and complete child, seen in full by her loving Daddy.

Standing on one foot, Rosie let her heart lead the way—like a dance or act of hope, balancing not by her own equilibrium but solely by God's. That is just what she did. Moving on her left foot, then her right—and back again. She got in a rhythm and she poured out thanks, hope, and adoration. In the process, the Spirit was setting her free. Every move she made seemed to say, *Finally, I am free to be me—and fear can no longer tackle me.*

If she didn't know where she was, she might have thought she was twirling on a beach. Letting go of people, of herself, of her environment, and just dancing with God. Endlessly breathing deep. Feeling light. Undoing her defenses bit by bit, stroke by stroke. Rejoicing in the brilliance of a setting sun. Splashing God's brilliance everywhere. Untethering worship and unleashing awe. She painted. Following Spirit and displaying glory.

This is the place where following God gets easy. It is where we pull out that little girl and say to her, "I remember you. You are good enough just as you are—just as God made you."

It is where we smile and unearth those small dreams we once had. And maybe, just maybe, we toss away all the standards and parameters and say, "Yes, God, I will go. I can because You can. I will paint Your glory."

### The Problem with the Rosie Story

If the Rosie story ended here, things would be so tidy. I have such a need for tidy sometimes, don't you? But here is the deal: tidy never brought restoration, not once, not ever, not even for a single person. So I am going to forgo that need and admit something to you.

I get jealous of Rosie. I look at her and think, *Wow, doesn't she have a story? Mine stinks.* I remark, "She is so artistic. I can't draw a cat without it looking like a mouse."

I hate to say these things; I know how bad they make me look. I mean, really? Who is jealous of a woman without arms? Me, apparently. Yuck.

Around Rosie, at times, I've wanted to clam up. I've wanted to hibernate. I've wanted to show off to make myself feel better. I've wanted to boast and brag. Yuck again.

Rosie is a risk to my status. She is a star that makes me feel like a speck of dust in a vast solar system. I get angry at her about that (as if she were responsible).

118

Somehow her strength makes me feel weak. Her vision makes me seem visionless. Her calling makes me feel less called.

But our calling doesn't disappear as we see another's calling appear. Perhaps, sometimes, it even emerges stronger.

One star in the night—that is good, it is worth seeing. But the brilliance of many stars, shining bright together? That is called "Whoa! Holy cow. Look at that. Stop and see, y'all!"

God never said that because one person shines another can't. He never said that because one has talent another won't. He never noted that He has a favorite child, either.

Remembering this brings me some solace, but of course I want more.

By now, you all know how I am ready to be done with this kind of junk. I know it is far more flesh than Spirit. I know I shouldn't be this way. I know it isn't helping. I know it probably pushes Rosie and me away from each other. I know she is doing great things for God and speaking to others and showing the brilliance and magnificence of His name in staggering ways. I get all this. I applaud this.

But sometimes my heart is ten steps behind my head. And being sure of how to fix myself, beyond banging my head against a wall, sometimes seems impossible to figure out in the moment.

Until the sword of the Spirit hits me like this: "Now that you have purified yourselves by obeying the truth so that you have sincere love for each other, love one another deeply, from the heart" (1 Pet. 1:22). It can't be that simple, can it? Is it simply about loving? If I love when I want to hate, will my heart finally feel great? It seems impossible.

But maybe it's not. Because what I've come to find out is that the Holy Spirit is a love dumper. The love we pour out, the Spirit dumps back in us (Rom. 5:5). The Spirit keeps giving. I keep getting. *I can do this. Yes!* It's far less about my strength and far more about His.

119

I figure it's worth a shot. It's better than ruining a friendship. So I thank God for Rosie. I praise Him that she is making His name known. I ask Him to expand her ground to share His story. I encourage her. I delight in her work. I ask God to open doors for her. I ask Him to bless her. I love her. I try something different.

And, surprisingly, what happens is more love pours out. Not only to her but also abounding in me. Somehow what I thought she would take from me, God replenishes. I get more than I ever wanted by wanting to love her.

It's interesting. It is so polar-opposite from what I expected. It's genuine love. It creates something. Together we need and help each other. We become warrior sisters in Christ rather than opponents in battle. We exalt Christ's name even higher. We see beyond darkness to the light He wants to bring to this world. We are empowered. We are emboldened. We are restored in deep ways.

And we find that the one we thought wanted to rip us apart is actually the one God uses to put us back together again. We delight and look over to our Chief and say, "We always thought it was about something else. Now we see it is all about love. Your love sets us free. And through that love, our unhinged creativity and unique personalities set others free."

He nods and lifts His own picture; it looks like beauty and community, unity and abilities splashed together in ways we never considered could work out. But they do. And He hangs it. We admire it. So do others.

What people stop to stare at, what they step back to ponder, is an image of Christ that is drawn by the movement of the Spirit who is very much alive. We are part of it. It is beautiful. It is Rosie. It is me. But it is better than our individual efforts. It is Jesus against the contrast of our flesh.

What is the Spirit longing to move you to? What is it only you were created to paint, with God? Have you given it a chance to flow?

Push everything—all voices, pressures, and demands—aside and let your Creator resketch your scenery. What you might see is your very image coming to life, where all of a sudden, Mary Poppins–style, you jump into the painting, Christ in hand and full of vibrant dreams, heartfelt beliefs, a raging need for justice, heart-strong inclinations of mercy, and passionate plans to spread love. You paint when you never thought you could draw worth a lick. It astonishes you.

But what you will realize is, you are not living in imaginary lands; you are living in truth, in the here and now. So you grab your newfound joy. You skip and you jump and you look for the other kindred hearts—and you celebrate. You thank God, for you no longer feel like a thankless shadow-chaser. You can't believe all you now have.

## *Something to Chew On*

### Speaking Courage

Tell me it's impossible and, with God, I'll say, "It's not."

Say no one can do it, and I will say, "If I believe it, and He wants it, God will see it through."

Remind me of my failings, and I will say, "They are just the start of new beginnings."

Speak of my faults, and I will say, "I may not be perfect, but I'm being perfected."

Come down on my issues, and I will say, "Today I fell, but tomorrow I'll rise."

Point out my problems, and I will say, "These are the schoolrooms for my triumphs."

Remind me of all the bad, and I will say, "The downpours are just precursors to rainbows."

Tell me all hope of light has vanished, and I will say,
"It is darkest before the dawn."
Taunt that I will never get better, and I will say, "I
may feel blind today, but I've got sight straight
up and through eternity tomorrow."

What words might you need to hedge in your new
bravery?

# *nine*
# Waiting While Trembling

## *I Don't Know What Will Happen (But I Know It Can't Be Good)*

Waiting for God is not laziness. Waiting for God is not going to sleep. Waiting for God is not the abandonment of effort. Waiting for God means, first, activity under command; second, readiness for any new command that may come; third, the ability to do nothing until the command is given.

G. Campbell Morgan

There is this time in life—I think just about every woman hits it. It's a time, probably not too long after all the strangeness of puberty, where you say, "Am I really going to make it out okay?" It seems pivotal. It's the moment you realize that life went from all safe and sound to blaring and scary. It's just about at this point that torment starts to plague you.

Don't tell me you don't know what I am talking about!

It usually starts out with some first love who left you. Or some prom date who stood you up. Or some newfound idea of beautiful that frizzed out of control before you had a second to brush your hair straight and rescue it. Or some timely insult that ruined your moment of glory. Or some name-calling that marred you forever.

Whatever it is, you stare in the mirror, tears falling, saying, "I thought life was better than this!" But it really isn't. Without Christ, and without all those detailed pages of hope written by His Spirit—nope, life doesn't get too much better. It just doesn't. It doesn't feel pretty. And even if you are pretty, you still don't feel pretty, because you never really believe it anyway. We are all chasing a mirage.

Anything but Jesus is one, really.

All this talk? It makes me want to silently get hopeless, maybe head to my closet and hibernate, but like I said, Jesus is the hope. Hope that is intended for our good and not for evil (Jer. 29:11). Hope that is with us (Ps. 46:7) and for us (Rom. 8:31) and all around us. He's got all this stuff near us that is good—or so "they" say, and so everyone says but me. I hate that I often don't believe. I nod, I agree—but inside, I don't really believe that well that God is always good. What I do well is fret.

As you know, it's a problem I'm working on.

The reality is, I can't stop thinking, *What if tomorrow's a wreck? What if what I don't know does kill me? What if women really are as mean as I think they are? What if World War III breaks loose while I am sleeping? What if I really have to get a root canal and the online dentist I found is really just a malpractice lawsuit waiting to happen? What if the house catches fire tonight? What will I do—do I know the escape routes? Better add these questions to the running list.*

When you're a disaster-hunter like me, it is hard to find yourself, your future, and your God when all you can think about is what might unhinge.

I've come to realize that good looks can't win God over, and neither can intelligence or funniness or whatever it is we use to tell ourselves we are loved enough. And if none of that works, what are we really to do? What is there, really, about me that will make Him—or anyone, for that matter—want to stay near?

I am not impressive enough to hold attention. I don't say this in a poor-me way, I say this in a getting-real-with-you kind of way. Even more, if I was God, I might leave me too, if the whole world was breaking down. I might leave for the bigger cause, for the real masses in pain, for world peace, but I probably would never desert world catastrophe for the likes of me.

Do you feel like you aren't enough to be loved? To be rescued?

## Searching for Love

My life has been a hunt for love—and isn't that really true for all of us? We often go from searching for it in a man to demanding it later from our husband or friends, and then to attempting to fill in the gaps with overcompensations for our every fear. It is like we throw a whole bunch of strategies up in the air and hope that one will fall just right.

*Please, God, please. Let it happen this time.*

At this time in my life, I searched and I searched hard. I headed to church. I headed to the bars. I roamed from here and there, hoping that Mr. Prince Charming was about to become my boyfriend/ husband in T-minus-one second. My worst nightmare looked like being alone my whole life—not because being alone is bad but because I would have to live as just me, with only my thoughts to help me. We know where that would end: disaster.

I couldn't let that happen. So I went on "missions." I'd snag a guy, get to know him, and then give up, knowing it was all his fault. When I didn't do that, I'd overexert myself to make up for the fact that I had no cruddy idea if the guy actually liked me.

125

Bar after bar, bliss in a glass never showed up, and I always felt cruddy the next day. Each attempt hurt.

### Failed Strategy #1

So I did what any self-respecting, righteous Christian girl would do: I worked harder for love. I did more church things and did them well, thinking God would get reciprocal in nature and hand out what I needed. I did this to no avail, and with no ring. Fortunately I got to the point where I realized I couldn't really work to earn something that Jesus already bought and paid for. I now know this is why Jesus said, "It is finished" (John 19:30).

### Failed Strategy #2

So on I went. Clearly I was learning other people had no power to help me. I had to regain control so as to be in control. I restricted my diet, believing that the world was right—to be thinner is to end up a winner. *Let's try it*, I figured. But I didn't end up a winner; all I did was prevent myself from being able to think straight. I lived in a fog where breathing, thinking, and relaxing felt horribly uncomfortable. I hurt.

### Failed Strategy #3

What do you do when your best strategies to prevent disaster fall like five loaded juggling balls directly onto your face? What do you do when you can't seem to keep life up in the air, where you are untouchable and where people don't get hurt?

These were always my questions. Sometimes they still are. Many days I still yell, "Ow!" and look up at God, like, *Why me?* But through all this trial and error, all this learning, all this disaster in my life, something gets worked out. And then, when lucidity sets in, the message appears more obvious: until we realize we can never do enough, we'll never live enough by the real strength that saves.

Hmm. This kind of knowledge sits well in my head. But it doesn't always last in my heart. At least not until my soul gets here, to this place: "God, I am not so good and I don't know what to do about it. Please rescue me." This kind of prayer is the equivalent of progress.

It attaches to our heart and makes its way, like oxygen, to every part of our limbs. It moves us differently. The second we say "I can't" to God, He steps in to show us His "I can."

I tried it. I tried it with the knowledge that God's rescuing horses are just around the corner. What if you tried it too? Just think: What might happen if you called on Him, waited on Him, hoped in Him, and believed in Him? If you started to activate those horses with belief in God's real power?

It will work. See disaster? Scream, "I am not so good. I don't know what to do. I can't. Come, God, rescue me!"

Then watch the cavalry come stampeding in, ready to move mountains because of just a miniscule seed of faith (Matt. 17:20). It won't always be as you demand or according to your timeline, but it will be. It will be done according to the One who holds the earth together. It will be done with love.

After trying 101 other strategies, I have come to believe this is the only way. A tree falling nearly directly onto my car: the only way. Birthing a baby in nearly thirty minutes with back labor, protruding head, and no meds: the only way. Feeling like the airplane was fizzling to the ground and was going to crash: the only way. Trusting God was all I had left when I felt like nothing else was left. It is the only way when things look their worst and disaster waits to strike.

The only way.

It is all we have left when the world gets meaner and uglier and we fear we might not be the ones left standing (which we always will, by the way; imagine my fist-bump to eternity).

This is prayer that works. And not only does it work but it also uplifts, especially when you couple it with "Thank You."

Thank You, God, that You will rescue me.

Thank You, God, that You are faithful to save.

Thank You, God, that You are the great I AM who will do what You say You will do.

When we say thank you we start believing we have a lot to be thankful for. We start seeing a whole bunch of good being worked out for us. It's a crazy thing.

I prayed this wild prayer and God started His work. He led me to a new church in the sunshine of California, Mariners Church, and it was here He started me on an adventure.

Somehow, to my surprise, I got pulled into going on a retreat nearly my very first day in attendance. I wasn't so sure what I was doing or where I was going, but I had prayed this prayer and I was going to see it through.

The only problem was that my friend Eating Disorder (otherwise known as ED) came with me. We hadn't really settled that love-feud yet. I was still hunting, after all.

But while at that retreat, Jesus grabbed me by the heart, people grabbed me by the hand, and my new eyes grabbed new truth. I was embraced, and I saw and felt things like I never had before. Deep mending. Broken stitches were pulled back together. An invitation to more was standing right before me and a wild call to wholeness sent by a loving God was surfacing. I wanted to open it. It was something, maybe something too easily described as love. But this something was far beyond love I'd known. It wasn't a man—well, I guess it was. It was Jesus.

He blew my mind.

Things were going well, almost too well there. And I know, *I really know*, that you all know, as fellow recovering-fearers, what we start thinking when "things are going too well," yes—*Trouble is brewing*.

And it was. ED wanted to go home. He wanted to ditch the people, the beautiful midnight walk to the little creamery up in the mountains, because he didn't feel "comfortable" about it. I should have told him to clam up, but instead I let him walk me home—to hide out from Jesus and all His followers. Couldn't have ice cream after midnight!

I crunched leaves underfoot and silently cursed ED. I hated what I was doing, especially when I had felt so much, learned so much, and drawn so close to God. ED, though, he said, *Don't think too much about it; we know what we have to do; carry on.*

God remembered my prayer, I believe. He didn't give up on it. I heard something in my heart as I walked. It trumped ED's voice of despair. And it sounded like, "The LORD himself goes before you and will be with you; he will never leave you nor forsake you. Do not be afraid; do not be discouraged" (Deut. 31:8).

I liked the thought. It settled me down. What I heard inside was, *Turn around—and stay around places where God is.*

And so I did. I got back on His path. I ate ice cream. I left ED behind. I met my man, Jesus Christ—and my other man, my husband-to-be. God walked me right up to meet my future on that late-night walk to a sky-high ice-cream parlor. Boy, did it all taste good.

Sure, it won't always happen so spic-and-span like this, but sometimes God just wants to show off, I think.

The truth is, the Lord is always looking; He is searching the earth for those whom He can trust (2 Chron. 16:9). He is seeking women who hear His voice. The ones who can leave the land of "impending tragedy" to risk it all for lands of "Discovering Victory."

Let them be *us*!

It doesn't happen overnight, nor should we demand that it does. It is a gradual process and a making, a building, and a progressing into more. God designed it like this; let's live it this way. Because the joy is found in the discovery of God—and there is no greater thing than perpetually landing yourself flat, face-first, right smack-dab in the center of it. It seeps in to fill every hole, or fear, in us.

Sure, it feels like waiting, but it is all about abiding. Every single, solitary day it is about abiding. Which means putting matters of God over matters of assuaging our restless mind. Which means finding a meeting place with God and determining to carpool together to the great places He is taking us, even if He detours to what seems like a bazillion rest stops along the way—which also means knowing that He will bring us through catastrophe to eternity, even if the worst disaster takes form.

Deep breath. He has you. Let your muscles relax. He can't, by the very makeup of who He is, slam the door in your face and leave. And He won't put His hands on His hips and say, *I am going to hit you where the sun don't shine. I am sick and tired of you.* He wants you.

Got it?

Sure, balls might drop, but either God will catch them before they hit or He will let them hit with the power of internal or eternal restoration. Let this settle in. There is a plan—and it always amounts to restored love.

With this, I am done with keeping all God's balls in motion. I have decided to say no to trying harder and say yes to God.

*Come, God—rescue me!*


## The Faithful Waiting Game

Imagine, thousands of years ago, standing there with the chosen apostles. You affectionately gaze at Jesus. Your all-in-all, your one and only, the best and most prized possession . . . except for one thing: Jesus is leaving you. Ascending.

*Now, Jesus—really?*

Everything in you wants to hug Him, pull Him close, and hang on to Him, saying, "Don't go! You can't. What will happen to me?"

You nearly do it. You kind of try, but before you can latch on, your attempt is halted, literally clouded over (Acts 1:9). You almost scream out, "No! Don't go!"

130

But you don't. You just stare, mouth agape, mind wondering, devoid of words.

You watch Him. You maybe tear up. You lose your breath for a minute.

> They were looking intently up into the sky as he was going, when suddenly two men dressed in white stood beside them. "Men of Galilee," they said, "why do you stand here looking into the sky? This same Jesus, who has been taken from you into heaven, will come back in the same way you have seen him go into heaven." (vv. 10–11)

My reply? It would have been, "I don't want to wait. I had what I needed and now it is gone. I have to wait for His 'something else'? No thanks. I will take back what I had. I mean, look what happened to Jesus. What will happen to me in the meantime? Who will come after me now? What might happen?"

I might even have tried something dumb, like jumping up so I could catch a corner of His robe before He was entirely gone, screaming, "I'll grab You, then You won't leave," but I don't think that would have gone over too well.

I wonder, though, if I might have remembered Jesus's words. It is His Word that makes a difference.

"Wait for the gift my Father promised . . . the Advocate, the Holy Spirit, whom the Father will send in my name, will teach you all things and will remind you of everything I have said to you" (v. 4; John 14:26).

Maybe this would have provided some hope. Hope that there was someone else coming to advocate for me. That there was someone who was going to teach me everything Jesus said. Wow. Would I have believed? I wonder.

Jesus loves blind faith. He loved the robe-clenchers, the feet-washers, the head-resters, and the perfume-wasters. He was into those who just grabbed the hem of hope—and waited.

He loves it when we get clingy. We cling to someone we love. We trust them too. Like we ask our children to trust us. Like we trust a lifeguard to save us. Like we trust a surgeon to heal us. Like we trust a paramedic to revive us.

We know we are really trusting when we feel okay with what He says.

This is the real-deal kind of thing, not perfect but unrestrained and unhindered trust in what we cannot see. It begins when our heart just starts wanting it and makes mini-strides in it. He understands this; it doesn't all drop on us overnight. Ask Him for it; He answers.

I think it is vitally important, because to believe is to relieve the tension of what is to come. You hand over your will and then rest arrives.

It is relieving.

Of course, it's not easy. Sitting and twiddling thumbs, abiding and trusting—this is graduate-level spiritual stuff. It is not easy—but then again, it is. Maybe the real problem is that we think it is far too easy, so easy it couldn't actually work.

It's sitting. Remembering. Thinking of Jesus.

Letting love settle. Truth marinate. Hope abound. Justice rise. Mercy work.

It's finally nailing shame to Jesus's cross. It's blessing God's master-planned community. It's knowing you are seen.

It is "Wait for the LORD; be strong and take heart and wait for the LORD" (Ps. 27:14).

What if we were to really believe that God's waiting ground is His best transforming ground? That each waiting ground we sit on will lead to a fireworks display of brilliance?

The New Testament has a story about that.

When the day of Pentecost came, they were all together in one place. Suddenly a sound like the blowing of a violent wind came from heaven and filled the whole house where they were sitting.

They saw what seemed to be tongues of fire that separated and came to rest on each of them. All of them were filled with the Holy Spirit and began to speak in other tongues as the Spirit enabled them. (Acts 2:1–4)

Who would have dreamed? God lit up the earth with the brilliant display of Holy Spirit! And in an instant, God is now within us. We walk with the very might and magnificence of God in our core. We are filled with His instruction. The Word of God brings power in our heart. We can worship in Spirit. Oh yes, Jesus knew He was leaving us His very best. No wonder He spoke so confidently.

Do we know this, too, that we've got His very best? We are privy to the deep things of God. Those kinds of wild things are being revealed to us. Can you even fathom this? It is right inside you.

It is our treasure and the box is unlocked and opened—waiting for us to plunder it. Not in a sinful way, but in an I-must-have-more kind of way. In a "Wow! This couldn't all be for me?!" kind of way.

You can't even begin to imagine the kinds of things being revealed. God's Word says, "The Spirit searches all things, even the deep things of God. For who knows a person's thoughts except their own spirit within them? In the same way no one knows the thoughts of God except the Spirit of God" (1 Cor. 2:10–11).

Spirit knows your wait.

Spirit knows your disaster plans.

Spirit knows your pains.

Spirit knows your sorrows.

Spirit knows God's heart toward you.

Spirit cares.

There is no plan to abandon you in the dry desert of unknown doom. There is no thought that you are too dumb, small, or odd-looking to be helped. There is no feeling that God's feelings have changed toward you.

God is—I Am. His Spirit is in you. Streams of living water pour out from inside your very self (John 7:38). This means you will always be sustained and nourished.

Let Him rush out from within you.

Is it setting in yet? How might your life change if you considered that the gap between what is and what is to come is where real deliverance is forged?

What might the Spirit be working in you so that you can arrive to places even greater than where you expected to land? How might you feel if you exchanged fretting for faith? What might that require you to do?

Remember, you're not sitting around; you are in the process of being found so you can go out and abound in Christ. Trust that!


### Waiting Well

Is there such a thing as waiting well? And how do we wait well when it feels like the hammer is going to fall or we'll be smacked by those falling balls again?

Here we go. The whole time I wrote this book, I kept wondering if it was going to be a disaster. I kept wondering if I was going to lay my heart out on a platter only to have it stomped all over. I had a real fear that this wasn't going to end well.

I kept on writing, though, and I kept on looking out the window, and what I kept on seeing were eagles. They were a little reminder to me not to keep my eyes on the worst—or the wait, or the process—but rather to keep my eyes on the heights of God. Heights that are called greater hope. This kind of hope works well in a wait, because "those who hope in the Lord will renew their strength. They will soar on wings like eagles; they will run and not grow weary, they will walk and not be faint" (Isa. 40:31).

*They will break their cages and escape.*

I love the sound of that (imagine me rubbing my hands together). I am hearing recovery, rest, and new strength sounding all through these words. I am hearing liberation and new declarations. Oh boy!

With this, it appears, if we make "hope" work, we can press into anything. Hope in God. Hope in His promises. Hope in eternity. Hope in the great vision of this thing called His glory being spread far and wide. It gets our eyes looking upon distances far beyond ourselves. It gets us some comfort. It is our way of escape.

We flap our wings, a feather drops, and we are off.

## Three Ways to Avoid Cry-Fests and Wait Well

### Wait Well Way #1

First, get your muscles strong—to endure and to fight—with hope. Train yourself to believe in the good thing God is working out on your behalf.

I love to watch those eagles out my window because they give me a new perspective of everything. They can see all the stuff we can't, from a viewpoint we don't have. And I don't know, but maybe they can see how all the dots connect between the points on the earth that seem so fragmented and broken to us. Who knows; I like to think about that though. I want to make sense out of the devastation and the tears and the people who are broken. I want nations and people and divisions reunited. Oh, how I long for that—and fret over what the evening news seems to warn me is coming. All that stresses me out and makes me wonder how it will end up, but what gives me calm is this:

> In a desert land he found him [he found us],
>> in a barren and howling waste [in the center of rubble].
> He shielded him and cared for him;
>> he guarded him as the apple of his eye,

> like an eagle that stirs up its nest
>> and hovers over its young,
> that spreads its wings to catch them
>> and carries them aloft. (Deut. 32:10–11)

After reading these words, my heart feels renewed. Maybe the eagles circle because they are keeping watch. And, just the same, God is keeping watch over me. He circles us because we are the "apple of His eye." He hovers over His young ones to keep us and to catch us when we fall.

### Wait Well Way #2

Second, thank God for every little thing He has done to protect you, to see you, and to guard you. Remember and actively praise Him in the moment for what He is likely doing.

You see, when you know you are covered, you know that you will make it out okay. Your perspective is crystallized, your vision gets farsighted, and you can start belting out tunes of joy that others are shocked—and longing—to hear. Your fight gets contagious. Its melody goes something like this: "Because you are my help, I sing in the shadow of your wings" (Ps. 63:7). Your attitude flips over.

### Wait Well Way #3

Third, let God's saving power give you an attitude adjustment. Sing. Praise. Get up and get moving right into what God is going to do for you.

If God is an eagle, we are His young. Young ones don't get left alone. They don't get pushed out of the nest before they are ready. God isn't pushing us around. He is on the ball, He is flying high, and He, simply, will not let us fall.

Knowing this, let's let these little decrees take flight:

*As I push beyond comfortable, God will fly me to unbelievable.*

*There is no sting of death under the very wing of God.*

*Nothing, no way and no how, can ruin a life God owns.*

## Something to Chew On

**Sometimes Science Speaks Louder Than Words:**
Have you heard of the marshmallow experiment? No, it is not an experiment proving the levels of wonderful your insides experience as you inhale the fresh, creamy sweetness of all things cocoa on a snowy day. (Although I believe that is an experiment worth noting.) What I am talking about here is a series of studies conducted in the 1960s by Stanford professor Walter Mischel.[1]

He told a bunch of toddlers not to eat the marshmallow he had given each of them. If they listened, they would get a second one, but if they didn't wait they would get no more. Then he left the room.

Guess what happened? Those wild and woolly rabbits went buck wild. Some, of course, didn't wait. But some listened and just sat, marshmallow in hand. Good holy-folk in the making.

These results are not what is staggering—what is staggering is how waiting seemed to be directly correlated to their future success, happiness, and progress.

The children who waited grew up to be adults who scored higher on the SATs, had less instances of substance abuse, were less likely to be obese, were better stress responders, were higher ranking socially, and scored better in life skills.

The best things come to those who wait, and those who wait find a better life—imagine that!

# *ten*

# Rejection and Opposition

## *They Have Issues*

Today you are you, that is truer than true. There is no one alive who is youer than you.

Dr. Seuss, "Happy Birthday to You!"

*S*he was an instant friend. You know the type, right? You meet and it's nearly love at first sight. She speaks your native language. She welcomes you with open arms. Her personality is like sweet tea on a sweet summer day. She nods up and down, smiles big, and says, "Let's be friends after this event." You nearly bat your eyes and reply, "It's a date" but catch yourself before your overzealous slip of the tongue. You have a feeling that God is ready to grow something amazing, and for once you want to see the flower unfold.

You can't wait to hold it and smile!

When I got home, I couldn't wait to message her. Good friends are like windblown dollars—you just have to reach out and seize them. This is what I have learned. I wasn't about to let her fly away. But I had to account for the dating-game-turned-mommy-game—the one that says you have to wait at least a day or two before following up. Can't seem too desperate!

Me: Hey, it was great to meet you. I can't wait to get to know each other more. (Fri. 9:24 AM)

Her: (Dead Air) (Viewed Fri. 10:00 AM)

Days pass.

Her: (Dead Air)

More days pass . . . more dead air.

Me: Hey! I am not sure if you got my message. Just checking back. I know how things can get lost in the shuffle. I can't wait to talk more. (Tues. 11:00 AM)

Her: (Dead Air) (Viewed Tues. 11:30 AM)

More days pass.

The more time passed, the more I was starting to pass her off as a rude, insensitive, selfish type. New thoughts surfaced. Did I even like this woman? What was even so great about her to begin with?

And why wasn't she answering me? It could only be one of two reasons: either her kids were intercepting my messages or she completely hated everything about me. *Wait! What if she really never liked me to begin with and I made a complete fool out of myself?*

The thought set in. *I am on her blacklist now; the one filled with all the crazy cuckoos and condemned ones, the ones who tried but didn't make the cut.* The ones who are now viewed as desperate and pathetic. The ones that all her real friends talk about. *What if she sees me like that?*

I could not let her see me like that. *Must. Save. Day.*

Me: Hey, just making sure you got this message? I wanted to follow up because we had plans to talk *(you meanie!).* (Thurs. 2:00 PM)

Her: (Dead Air) (Viewed Thurs. 2:30 PM)

With everything I had in me, I wanted to banish her to the endless circle of recorded customer service torture. *She should suffer for acting like this.*

Someone please save me from this insanity! The more I dug myself into the hole of rejection, the deeper I continued to dig, until I was so far in all I wanted anyone to do was to take the dirt and cover my head with it so I could hide, if only just for a little while.

A respite, so I didn't have to feel so horrible.

Have you ever felt like your outstretched hand, inviting intimacy, was smacked directly into your own face—leaving you with yolky, soggy, yucky, and drippy egg all over your face? Even more, did it ever convince you that you were actually standing in the center of your sixth-grade cafeteria while everyone else stared at you, wide-eyed and laughing?

*Look at her! She did that?!*

Rejection wags a finger, squints its eyes, and says, "Don't you worry; I'll be back again to get you." It's a bully.

We don't forget its threats so we live defending, arming, and guarding. We walk around with a shield and arrows at the same time. Our armor is emblazoned with the words *I will not be hurt again.* We get resolved and we:

1. Give a half-hearted effort to God's greatest opportunities for us.

2. Procrastinate and write off big dreams.

3. Self-condemn so when we're rejected we aren't shocked.

4. Give up in the now so we don't have to be rejected later.

5. Hurt others first before they can hurt us.

When we live with our arms wrapped around ourselves and ten-inch-thick layers of metal around us, love has a hard time making its way through. What love can penetrate your thick defenses?

## Low-Hanging Love

Wild truth: God's love is hanging right out there for you to grab. When I was in the world of business, people called things like this "low-hanging fruit," or an opportunity that, once seen, you'd best be wise to go grab and "eat it" before you miss it altogether. It's what smart people do.

Are you grabbing all God's low-hanging love?

Sometimes I do. Sometimes I don't. I want all of it, though, because when we are seized by His love we can't as easily get seized by other people's problems. Instead, we end up centered in the riptides of peace and passion and all that jazz. I want that. It's much easier than my song-and-dance show that tries to get people to give me what I need.

Do you do a little jig too—to get what you need? To try to get people to look your way? To maintain happiness? If so, what is it?

I understand. I do it all the time. I want to mother well and be cheered by some random onlooker at the grocery store. I want to write something really beautiful and be noticed for my flair. I want to sing and have the person next to me say, "Nice!" I want to come up with the perfect advice for you and hear you say, "Wow, Kelly, I never thought about it like that. It's exactly what I need to do!"

I want attention, validation, and recognition; I guess I always have.

I feel horrible for saying that.

But it's true. And the difficulty is that people mostly care only a half-iota about me and a whole heaping dollop about themselves. Leaving me feeling unseen, unworthy, and unloved.

It's at this point where I want to turn in for the night permanently—almost.

Until I remember there is a reason why I long to be adored.

I long to be adored because God made me to be adored by Him. I long to sing and dance because God created me to sing and dance—for Him. He delights over this kind of thing—when it is for Him, about Him, and with Him. My motivations aren't all wrong—but mostly my execution is.

Is yours?

He adores us. You heard me. I think this idea will scare some people; I don't care. I think some people are going to think we should only adore Christ. Yes, we adore Him first, but our need to be adored is not bad, it is intrinsic.

Take a look.

1. He delights over us with singing (Zeph. 3:17).
2. We are altogether beautiful in His eyes (Gen. 1:27; Song of Songs 4:7).
3. He knows us—our very frame; when we sit, rise, lie down, and speak (Ps. 139:1–4).
4. He knows the number of hairs on our head (Matt. 10:30).
5. He knows our every step (Job 14:16).
6. He has thoughts so vast toward us we cannot even begin to count them (Ps. 139:16–18).
7. He works in us for His pleasure (Phil. 2:13).
8. He loves us, independently of us (1 John 4:10).
9. He watches us—who we were, are, and will be (Prov. 15:3).

10. He knows our everything (1 John 3:20).
11. His thoughts are precious to us (Ps. 139:17).

Who are we to be adored? No one, really. But God made us with this desire because He desires to fill it. He sent Jesus to the cross because He loves us. He makes us worthy not by our merit but because of His—and He loves to see us enjoying, delighting, dancing, and living abundantly with Him.

Why do we fight it?

Fend off the shame, ladies. Fend off the guilt you feel because you want to be seen.

Go ahead, be seen! Be seen by God. Do your silly dance, sing your off-key song, and know that when you do, God cheers. Why? Because it is all for Him.

And maybe when you do, you'll feel something rise up in you. It will be pure, it will be real, it will be whole, it will be sweet, and it will be tender. Because it is that thing that you pushed deep down, figuring no one cared about it. It's that thing you locked up and called stupid. You make it live again.

When you do it for God, it isn't so stupid anymore. When you do it for Him it is radiant. So you do it. You let it go a little. You bring it out and, almost in an instant, you're teleported back to that sun-soaked beach. A beach where you simply are who you are and God is who He is. And you go about making your wild moves and exuberant tunes, and you move your hands and you twirl and let go. You come alive to the joy that is in you and the wind swirls around you. You become that little girl and feel the sand under your toes. You let her be; you let her sing and let her feel the sun and the heat of all-consuming love.

It brings you to life.

And this you know: you don't need timelines because you know that this moment is timeless. You don't need fanfare because Jesus is your fan. You don't need credit because all the credit goes to Christ on the cross. And you are okay with this.

Why?

Because all the rays around you confirm that the King sees you. He smiles over you and downright delights over you—and He always will (Ps. 37:4; 147:11).


## All Things Are Possible

Matthew tells us, "With God all things are possible" (19:26). And it's true—all things *are* possible with God. I am learning these aren't just clichéd words you throw out when that friend has a problem you can't quite sum up over a one-hour lunch. Nope. These are words that reach into your deep places, to heal up the gashes that no one else sees—or for that matter you don't even want to see.

You don't care to see because you have no idea what you are supposed to do with them. After all, it is much easier to put on some Neosporin and slap on a few Band-Aids rather than think of the surgery that might transpire if you got into really understanding them. *Get 'em gone*, you think. And sometimes that is your best and seemingly only course of action.

*When in doubt, avoid. When feeling the heat, defend. When in pain, hide.*

You get all ready to ink this stuff on yourself and call it your life tattoo—then call it a day. I have pretty much done that. But at this point I want to share with you, friends, that I really am starting to make some progress with this thing called fear fighting.

The whole idea of stop, drop, and roll comes back to mind. Remember that? It is where you stop to see, drop to your knees, and roll into the greatness and grand possibilities of God. I think it is important to bring up again here because when we start to think of what God can do and how His heart inclines toward us, we don't need to worry about those who seek to oppose and reject us. Before we know it, all those insults, cold shoulders, and aggravations fade.

I only say it because it works.

You start to hear a different truth resound within you. Things get real. You go from random thoughts of *God loves me* to enduring thoughts of *God can't stop loving me*, and from a passing moment of *God will get around to me* to feeling *God is simply all around me*.

From *God will one day propel me* to *Today, God compels me*.

Sure, you still see those people do very mean things from the corner of your eye, and you hear them too, but now you know that God is handling your impossible feelings. You can let your shoulders rest. You also know He is working all things out for your good (Rom. 8:28). Your existence doesn't feel so scary. You know that while you are still, He is fighting for you (Exod. 14:14). That relieves the pressure you want to inflict on others—and yourself.

You begin to like the sound of your voice.

This is called believing in possibilities. Believing that God can do all things. That His abilities transcend your feeling that you stink and will fail.

In this, you don't have to rely on the fleeting acceptance of others, because God's acceptance is rock solid. There's a big difference. Behold: you don't need from others what God has already given you.

It is powerful what happens when this conversion transpires within us—when we see by the eyes of Christ rather than the eyes of the world. Rather than witnessing a whole pile of smelly and steaming circumstances, we hear a voice of newfound strength rise up in us.

> I know that my redeemer lives,
>> and that in the end he will stand on the earth.
> And after my skin has been destroyed,
>> yet in my flesh I will see God;
> I myself will see him
>> with my own eyes—I, and not another.
> How my heart yearns within me! (Job 19:25–27)

We start to look at His power—risen, ruling, and not refusing us. The power of people's opinions diminishes.

The strength of rejection crumbles. It can't stand under the weight of Jesus's resurrection. He rose above the cross—and brings us with Him.

Knowing this, we rise from our chair and step up and out. We love.

We don't get pushed over by people anymore because we start speaking compassion and forgiveness to them. We start thinking of how we can bless the ones who have hurt us. We start thinking that what was meant to harm us is now used for good (Gen. 50:20). We are not trembling; we are fighting. We are pressing in to the greater possibility that will rise out of what others said would never happen. We see past people, places, and things to see God's things.

We become overcomers, no matter what.

*No!* we reply, if only in our head. *With God it can happen!* It can and we will not believe otherwise. *God is greater than any injury to me. Enemies fall before Him. People will bow down to Him. This person, circumstance, job demotion, or letter will not ruin me, for Christ has already made me.*

We fight. We fight with the confidence that Christ wins and will win every time.

This confidence is like shooting off a gun but one loaded with peace and humility. We don't need to get angry any longer, for what was stolen we can now see God is working to more than restore (1 Pet. 5:10).

What would happen if you were to walk through this world believing that not one grain of your worth, your call, or your identity depended on other people?

Because let me tell you something: it doesn't. Your worth is completely independent of every talking head or commentator or shunner or name-caller. It has nothing to do with any of them.

Sure, they will be part of the story, because they were part of Jesus's story and we can expect opposition, but we don't have to live shot down by them any longer.

What a wasted life if we settle for anything less! We don't want to reach the end of our days only to look back and say, "Oh, it's that guy's fault I did't live for you, Jesus. He rejected and opposed me."

I kind of fear Jesus might look at us and say, "Well, he rejected Me too—and guess what? So did you."

Whoops, Jesus! Sometimes I forget to see it that way.

How many times have we rejected Jesus?

Let's just see as Jesus sees. Of course He isn't out to point fingers at how we are all messing up. But I just don't want any chance that we might miss the point of life, friends. Get my heart, here.

We can't blame on others what is really a matter of self. *God, show us where we are wrong and lead us in your right ways.* By the way, this is another great prayer. One worth daily utterance.

This prayer moves doubters to lands once seen as impossible to reach. Nothing is impossible with God. His faithfulness works. His love heals the haters and always endures. His covenant of peace will last forever (Isa. 54:10). God doesn't tell us lies. God doesn't offer us bad advice. On the contrary, he leads us "in the way everlasting" (Ps. 139:24).

Will you move with the motion of His wind or will you fight it, your hair a windblown mess, like you always have?

He wants to push you to greater lengths—lengths that are indescribable but not impossible. Go. Don't look back. Don't look left or right. Don't get thwarted by swirling chatter. Just go. Go so that, one day, where you land is a place you never believed was possible. A place where you cheer, jump, and scream, "Look what He did! Look what He did!"

You arrive at your victory ground.

And everyone has to crane their neck to see what only God could have done for you.

## The Rejected Rising

Jesus looked at Peter and asked him for the third time, "Do you love me?"

I wonder if Peter, staring into those eyes he had grown to love, wanted to keep guilt close. I wonder, if through tears, he considered those three times he should have screamed, "Yes! Yes! Yes! This is my Lord! He is mine and I am His!" I wonder if he wanted to slap himself for his faulty love. I wonder if maybe he even considered avoiding Jesus altogether. I wonder if he was inclined to give himself new names, like doubter, loser, and failure.

Three times Peter failed. Three times Jesus asked.

There seems to be restoration here. A rebuilding. Would Peter accept it?

He did. He didn't let the rejection in his past reject Christ again. And he didn't allow his internal feelings of rejection to reject Jesus's attempts to love him. I want to learn from him.

Peter answered, "Lord, you know all things; you know that I love you" (John 21:17).

Peter realized God still wanted his love and that he still wanted God's. If you want to get healed, get to this truth.

Love liberates.

Jesus must have known progress was made. He replied, "Feed my sheep" (v. 17).

Underneath that simple command were other messages, I believe. Messages like:

"I felt rejected, but will I reject you, ever? I cannot."

"You might feel like you lost, but I never lost you. In fact, I found you so I can do great things with you."

Jesus speaks these things to us too. He says something like, *The Spirit is in you, because I want you. I have things for you to do.*

Peter's "thing" looked like building a church on a rock that even the gates of Hades could not overcome (Matt. 16:18). Wow!

Love compels.

If we really listen, I bet we'll hear our "things." Things like, *Through you I will do the impossible, the impractical, and the immense if only you believe and receive* (Isa. 14:27; Matt. 19:26; Luke 1:37).

God is calling us to receive His best things. But we have to open the door. We have to be willing to step out into places where we might get hurt. Where we fear rejection might be shot right at our heart. We have to go with Jesus and in the Spirit, knowing He will be our mind's protective armor. We cannot fear the prospect of losing our bad companion of fear.

## A New Helper, Propeller, and Mentor

It is hard to ever imagine Jesus saying it was better that He go, so "the Advocate" could come, but He did (John 16:7). I mean, who could be better than Jesus? It seems almost ludicrous to us.

Jesus took things a step further too; He said that with the Holy Spirit the disciples would have the ability to "receive power" to witness to the "ends of the earth" (Acts 1:8).

And there is that little word again. Did you see it? *Receive.* The word that means the opposite of reject, misunderstand, or refuse. We have the ability to receive the fullness of the Spirit and to send it out far and wide. Peter had that ability too—to receive or refuse.

For, as we already know, God was about to hit Peter with the full impact of the Spirit. A pressure, a power, a moving-in that would deliver strength and life-change. An indwelling that would transform him physically, emotionally, and spiritually. It is the kind of thing that we long for.

But, still, Peter had the real power to deny it. He could have missed the "sound like the blowing of a violent wind [that] came from heaven and filled the whole house where they were sitting" (Acts 2:2). He could have missed "what seemed to be tongues of fire that separated and came to rest on each of them" (v. 3).

This idea bothers me, probably because I suspect I miss the big things—or worse yet, inadvertently dismiss them.

What if Peter missed the confirmation of his real transformation, the sense of his real belonging, and his true vision coming alive because he denied the very words of Christ?

Wow. That thought scares me.

Just think about it for a moment. Yes, Jesus had spoken restoration, but Jesus was gone. And in the time between Jesus leaving and the Spirit arriving, Peter was very much the same man, in the same body, stuck in the same world.

Peter had a real chance to question everything. He had a real chance to misunderstand if he really was a vital part of it all. He had a real chance to dispute if God really meant what He said and said what He meant.

We have this real chance in our lives too. Don't we? Will we receive truth or renounce it?

Imagine how a grain of misunderstanding could have impacted Peter's reception of the Spirit. He might have thought, *I'm not that deserving of God's good stuff.* Or he might even have dismissed the moment with excuses. *Well, that was some heavy wind, but it couldn't have been anything more than that.* Or he might've misunderstood. *Jesus said I was a rock because I am stuck in my bad ways.* Or he might have refused with overhumility, saying, "I am not worthy! I am not worthy! Find someone else. You really don't want a mess-up like me."

He could have put a hand up to God.

I thank God that Peter didn't. I am so glad he took God at His Word. He could have missed so much.

But all this discussion gets me thinking. Do I let my thoughts declare my truth, or do I let God's? Because this small difference makes the difference.

If we dwell on our past rejections, we'll miss out on God's great projections working to make us well.

Peter laid down all his defenses and offenses, ignored the critical eyes of judgment around him (Acts 2:13), and *received*.

1. He abandoned his personal causes (selfishness, pride, and so forth).
2. He relinquished the past (he believed he was forgiven).
3 He absorbed the present (he knew God was around him).
4. He unapologetically chose to stand in the greatness Jesus had already promised (this is called *faith*).

It seems simple; but, then again, God never really said things have to be complex. Simple yokes for simple folks (Matt. 11:30; 1 Thess. 4:11).

Do you make things simple or complex?

Receiving is simply about being where God is. In our modern world this means that we

1. are aware, not distracted (with our iPhone, iPad, impressions, or own ideas).
2. are willing, not guarded (choosing worship and wonder all through our day).
3. are ready, not doubt-filled (praying and looking with expectancy to see and hear biblical truths come alive).
4. know all things are possible, not impossible (knowing God is acting for you even when others seem to be acting against you).

You see, when we get in the mindset of receiving, God blows us away with His giving.

Take a look at what happened with Peter: he rose up, emboldened, emblazoned, and empowered, and spoke like he never had before. He stepped into Christ's rock-steady promise, "on this rock I will build my church," not with his tail between his legs but forthrightly and without apology. Loudly he proclaimed:

> I see that the LORD is always with me.
>> I will not be shaken, for he is right beside me.
> No wonder my heart is glad,
>> and my tongue shouts his praises!
>> My body rests in hope.
> For you will not leave my soul among the dead
>> or allow your Holy One to rot in the grave.
> You have shown me the way of life,
>> and you will fill me with the joy of your presence.
>> (Acts 2:25–28 NLT)

When the face of Christ's courage comes alive, through the Holy Spirit, we start speaking all these wild, fearless declarations—and we actually believe them.

In fact, something starts gushing. What was spiritually dry becomes spiritually soaked, packed and dense with real flow; it has a strong enough current to ripple through the whole world. It's like the Spirit is lighting a match. We just let it strike us and then we step back and see with new sight. Others look, too, because fire draws people.

Let the Spirit revive you. Let His rivers of living water flow right out of you (John 7:38). For the Spirit is a love dispenser (Rom. 5:5). He fills us until we overflow, and what spills over gives a fresh drink to the thirsty, those just like us. Then the Spirit fills us up again, and again we overflow.

See the cycle?

We don't grow tired, the current doesn't stop, the energy is uplifting, and His love moves nations.

Peter proves this flooding phenomenon; we can see the tides of new life all around him. Just look at the results.

1. Three thousand people were added to the church in one day because of Peter's sermon (Acts 2:41).

2. The church was filled with peace and it was strengthened (Acts 9:31).

3. The church, in the comfort of the Spirit and by fear of the Lord, was multiplied (Acts 9:31).

4. Secret hearts were laid bare as people fell down to worship God, "exclaiming, 'God is really among you!'" (1 Cor. 14:25).

Rejection fades in the wake of the Spirit, because, frankly, nothing else matters but Him, when we are nearly face-to-face with God. We don't need words or affections or uplifting by other people. We focus on our first love and who He has called us to love.

It's called feeding His sheep.

It is not that you will never be rejected, because you will be. You will be rejected as that person laughs in your face for loving Jesus, you will be rejected when that person tells you that you shine too brightly for Christ, and you will be rejected when someone says, "You can't really believe that!?" Yes, you will, in fact, be rejected; you will be rejected time and time again, and then again. You will be opposed. But what also happens is, you don't so much care.

You know you are alive.

Rejection becomes of no consequence when you stand in the presence of the One transforming you into His beautiful image "with ever-increasing glory" (2 Cor. 3:18).

What comes alive is this: *all things are possible.*

What also surfaces are these decrees:

*What God can do is entirely independent of what others do.*

*The image of Christ allows me to reimagine all I can do with Him.*

*People can't steal what God has put in me.*

And you know it. Beyond anything else you know it. You know there is nothing that can come between you and that truth. You hold it tight.

But realize it is actually low-hanging love—love that you grabbed and held and savored with all your heart.

## Something to Chew On

**The Spotlight Effect:** Let me tell you something: you think about yourself far more than anyone else does. The Spotlight Effect proves it. Before you run wild with visions of yourself freaking out on stage while a crowd watches, this kind of study is far different. It proves that we are actually noticed and judged far less than we think we are.

While we are thinking, *She will hate my clothes*, that other girl is probably thinking something along the lines of *She will hate my shoes*.

Or while we feel our sweaty armpits, our interviewer is probably feeling his hungry stomach.

While we are thinking that everyone is noticing how we are stumbling over our words, everyone is probably noticing how our point is making a lot of sense.

*Expect the best.*

*Extend yourself grace.*

*Enter the door of expectation. The next of God's best things awaits you there.*

Rejection becomes of no consequence when you stand in the presence of the One transforming you into His beautiful image (2 Cor. 3:18).

## *eleven*
# The Past

*I Hate That Place. Let's Not Talk about It.*

Oh yes, the past can hurt. But you can either run from it or learn from it.

Rafiki, The Lion King

The past ain't no easy thang.

There is a story. It goes like this. There was a dad. He had a daughter. One day she got herself beautiful and she looked in the mirror. She saw her round face and noticed her abundant freckles, but this day things didn't look so odd, so weird. So out of place. In a way, she felt like she was growing into herself. She saw something new. Something special, even.

She stood in front of the mirror and brushed her auburn hair. Today it shone. Today she felt good. She grabbed the new dress she hadn't yet worn and put it on. It looked spectacular.

She spun in the mirror, a small smile breaking through.

*Where's Daddy? Wait till he sees me!*

She ran outside. Her dad sat on the patio, flowers around him, drink on the table, peaceful and calm. He would see her and admire her for sure. He would accept her this day.

She ran up and jumped onto his lap.

"Get off me! Just get off!" He screamed and pushed her off his lap. He howled loud and looked at her in pain.

She stood, not knowing what she had done, and not feeling loved but rather entirely injured.

She cried. She broke. She didn't understand. What was seared in her was the disapproval of her daddy and the feeling she would never be enough. Her arms fell. She was devastated and destroyed.

Then and there, she decided she was unworthy.

When her dad regained his composure, he looked at her and said, "Somehow, two bees got caught between us and stung me."

She didn't know what to think. His reaction had nothing to do with her. But still, she felt wrecked. He'd dissed her.

As time went on, what settled in was bitterness and anger. She knew he hadn't meant to hurt her, but he still had.

Now she would have to live with that horrible memory plaguing her again and again. She would have to wonder if every man would push her away. Whenever she felt good, she'd suspect it was about to be ruined. That things were going to explode. That people would push her away.

That she was unworthy.

Thirty years later, unintended slights still bother her greatly.

The past is no easy thing to untangle. There are so many people and parts and perspectives to it—it can seem completely overwhelming and it can be difficult to erase emotion. It can feel hard to figure out.

To figure out:

*Others*. People who think they did no wrong.

*Our innocent selves*. People who suffered the brunt of it and maybe have no fault in it.

*Our guilty selves.* Ones certainly at fault in some way.

*God.* The One who didn't stop it.

Where is your past still tangled?

## Calling the Weary Folk

Feeling broken by yesterday?

I think everyone is, in some way. No matter how impressive and incredible any family was, there still remain childhoods full of hurts. No one is perfect; people are injured and life is rough. This is earth, after all, and there is no avoiding pain. It can sit heavy on God's kids—for a long, long time. *Is it hopeless?* we ask. *Will we ever get over it?*

I find relief in knowing God doesn't tell us to wrap it up with tinsel and call it a day, or to get out the broom and brush it to places unseen. Nope. He tells us to *come*, as in, "Come to me, all you who are weary and burdened, and I will give you rest" (Matt. 11:28).

*Come settle down with Me.*
*Come hear My heart toward you.*
*Come unveil your sorrows.*
*Come and hear what I whisper.*

This is the part of the equation I usually skip in an effort to jump ahead to the bottom line, where I just push through and make it out okay. I hardly ever do. Yet the Spirit wants to step in and stop us midleap, if we let Him. He readies and renews a heart that is listening (Eph. 4:23; 1 Cor. 2:10). Those who come and nestle up for the day next to the Savior, ready to receive His words of new vision, will be given rest. They get to tune in to God's love.

God knows all the angles of your story. It doesn't really matter so much from which perspective you stand—bitter because you were misunderstood, judgmental, angry at God, or looking to sin to ease the deep cavities left from abuse—His compassion blankets everything. He knows. He knows just what each of us needs.

The problem for me is that I like to have a plan, and this whole idea seems vague and unknown. Risky. It seems arduous and agonizing to dig deep. It's far easier just to rush into what lies before me and pretend that the past is the past.

Yet God sends a gentle reminder to my rushing soul that sounds like this: *You don't have to see it all as sunflowers and rainbows, My child* (Gal. 4:6). *I would call that faking it, and I've never been one for lies. If I am a God of truth, then I already know your truth and can handle it. Lay it on Me. I carried the world on the cross, after all. So come, hand it over; unburden yourself and let Me carry it. Take it off and I will fill you with something new that will undo you to peace.*

Somehow His way seems easy, not patronizing or aggravating, and that is what I am really after. Hmm.

There is real charge behind it. It gets me understanding that God really is good and full of understanding. It gets me understanding what lies beyond the hump called, "I am angry and can't get over it." It gets me seeing beyond all the stuff that has blocked my view of God. I like this. I like it a lot.

Because it's only at this point that I could say something so wildly extravagant as, "Praise be to the LORD, to God our Savior, who daily bears our burdens" (Ps. 68:19).

And to really know it as truth.


### Remember Neena?

Do you remember my friend Neena? We talked about her and the devil not so long ago.

When we left her, earlier in the book, she had a gun pressed against her temple. She had been raped, abused, battered, demoralized, and negated her whole life.

So much of her past was not her fault. So much of her past was actually the fault of other people's bad pasts. This happens.

I wish I could erase that pain from her mind sometimes. I wish I could just go back and power-punch the criminals who hurt her. I can't even imagine what it was like to be her. Waiting. Anticipating. Agonizing. Knowing that your very existence was hated. Knowing that one gunshot would end it all. Knowing that your own child could suffer in the crossfire. How does one live with trauma like this?

It burdens me. It angers me. It ticks me off.

What ticks you off? It says a lot.

You see, what ticks you off is often tightly tethered to your trauma.

Maybe not in the exact same capacity, but perhaps because of the same outcome of feelings. Feeling powerless. Feeling shamed. Feeling pained. Feeling taken advantage of.

Let that sink in, and then let's move back to Neena.

With a gun pressed against her head and her emotions running wild, her heart fluttered and her face reddened—but then, something happened. Something miraculous! The safety jammed and the gun failed to fire.

I can't imagine her begging, cajoling, or pleading. I can't imagine what her mind must have thought when she heard no gunshot, or the relief that must have flooded her as she and her baby got away scot-free. They made it. She made it.

But did she?

What you seem to escape in a moment is often not so easily avoided over a lifetime; those images replay forever. They keep going and going on auto-play and, I'll tell you, it never looks like a picture of escape. Instead, it always plays out like a film of capture.

Neena replayed and replayed, until she was certain revenge was the only way. She loaded a gun. She put it against his head and tried her hardest to imagine the sound it would make. *Bang!* She wasn't about to live this nightmare anymore.

What past are you always trying to kill? How does it replay? Injure you? Hold you back?

Now, if you're the type that wants to say, "Nope! Not me. I don't do that," let me tell you something: if you numb, kill, or run from your feelings, you can be certain you are living in the past. Here are some examples:

You limit your eating to control your surroundings.

You overeat to quell loneliness.

You cut down your spouse to feel stronger.

You push family away when you need help.

You spend unlimited dollars to hide an empty internal closet.

You sidestep the truth so you can keep on _____.

You dull the pain by inflicting pain.

You hand out abuse because you feel abused.

You manipulate people to get your deepest needs met.

You drink hard after a hard day of existence.

You seek love to feel loved.

You buy "happy," no matter the cost.

You get selfish to make yourself feel good again.

Normally, these present actions are forged through past beliefs: what you lived through as a child will replay as an adult.

Maybe you felt you had to fight to win, defend to be safe, keep your feelings hidden, be perfect so you weren't abandoned, make others always feel good, or fix everything.

What was it for you?

Without Jesus, what you spend your life trying to run away from nearly always captures you in the end. What you most fear, if left untended, is what tends to draw near.

Same injuries. Same type of people. Same circumstances. Somehow we are drawn to it. We have been conditioned to expect it so we re-create it.

Don't throw up your hands now and shut down, my friends. The situation is not hopeless.

If you change those past beliefs, you can change your current actions—or rather, your reactions—and then, through Christ, you can change your life.

This is what I am finding. This is what fear fighting is all about. We are redoing those faulty neurons that fired when faulty things happened to us in our past. We are digging out old beliefs that lead to quick-fire responses and replacing them with new love that leads others to find new love all for themselves.

Coming to God is vital for this kind of work. Here is where He whispers and helps you grasp all kinds of new revelations that the Spirit receives directly from God and sends to you like a personal love letter.

Neena wasn't at this point yet, but all I can say is, she didn't pull the trigger. I figure this was a very, very good decision. A very good decision amid many poor decisions—decisions to hurt herself, to damage others, to follow witchcraft, to be a man's doormat, and to live in anger.

We can't entirely blame her. But still, Neena the abused turned abuser. Neena the injured decided to injure. Neena the punching bag for anger became angry. What we most detest, we can easily become—if we aren't constantly choosing to believe a very good God has very good plans for us.

## Surprise!

I have a surprise for you all. Don't you love a good surprise? I do! Here goes: I love Neena. I love, love, love her. She is my dear, dear friend.

I am so proud of her too! You want to know why? Today she lives much more like a mascot for this book than she does a doormat for the abusers. I want to dress her up—all Fear Fighter—and let you see her walking around as the warrior woman she really is, with fists up, a wide grin, and love oozing out. You would smile so big. You would high-five her. You might even want a picture with her.

You see, this woman is more a fighter than any champion boxer ever could be. Why? She heard the word *come* and she walked her bloodied and beaten self right on over to His throne, bruises and all. She sat down next to Him and let Him minister to her wounds.

She was just herself and God just Himself—and that was enough. He could see her, and she was okay with that.

I am so glad Neena didn't listen to those old, replaying words of *blah, blah, blah* that sounded a lot like, "You bad, bad girl. Look at how you messed things up now. You will never be okay. God will never forgive you." There is no doubt that those words tried.

But she didn't listen; she didn't stay stuck. She pushed past them. This is the power of "Come." It looks a whole lot like a daughter running to her Daddy. Sure, she might feel afraid she is bothering Him or annoying Him, but she does it anyway, and asks Him how He feels toward her. And she listens. This is when He tells her His truth. She hears it because she really wants to know.

Her Daddy says little things to His daughter. He says:

*You can do it!*

*Don't forget who I made you to be.*

*The Spirit I gave you does not make you timid but gives you power, love, and self-discipline* (2 Tim. 1:7).

*Hold on to My truth and you won't be shouldering lies.*

It is at this point that His daughter normally runs into His arms and says, "Daddy, I am so, so, so sorry for all these things I have been keeping from You." Some sort of great power gets restored after an infection like this is removed. She gets healed.

No doubt, this happened with Neena. She got receptive and God got active. Today, she walks with King Kong–like steps of weighted courage. She shakes the ground. She speaks from experience. She changes hearts and shifts mindsets. It is God in her. It is His victory surfacing in her heart and toward others. It is new beliefs that pour out. They speak testimony, validity, and God's great ability to change everything in the blink of an eye.

It sounds like this: *Jesus saves. Jesus rules. Jesus wins.*

I can't help but think that when we let forgiveness work in us, it starts to work out something new through us. I love that! New passions and new sorts of relationships rise to the surface of our life. The things we are doing look all new and all kinds of exciting.

What I also love about Neena is that she isn't angry, except at evil. She's also a whole lot of fierce now. She prays with so much power that, if you prayed with her, you'd want to lie down before God because her words give you an idea of how powerful He is. She pulls her soul out and lays it on the carpet. She is undone and unafraid. She is strong in the face of fear. And, with all of this, I am pretty confident she makes the devil shake in his boots. After being with Neena you know you are just a little bit stronger and your vision of Jesus is just a little bit bigger. She has that effect on people. She rubs off.

I have joked with her that I want to have her as a bobblehead on my dashboard so that when I get down in faith, she can start spouting prayer filled with Scripture that will move mountains. I was kidding—kind of.

All other things aside, I praise God that Neena didn't let who she was define who God really made her to be. She could have, you know?

She could have stayed stuck. She could have been ruined. She could have killed and destroyed lives. She really could have.

But she chose to stand and be made new, with new beliefs. Will we?

Neena inspires new decrees:

*Past victories are the makings of future ministries.*

*What didn't kill you yesterday has no real power to kill you today.*

*It's no longer about the one who hurt you but He who is ready to heal you.*

*What you hate about yourself, God stands ready to love away.*

## Bludgeon Her (or Yourself)!

The guilty one. She stood. Did creation pause? Did it stop with the high drama of the moment? Did people's mouths go agape at the sight of her, the vile one?

Her secrets were no longer secret; her dirty laundry flew high. Every look marked her low worth. She shivered. She knew what was to come—what she deserved.

How could she ever forgive herself for all the affairs, the lust, and the longing? Who knows, maybe each stone thrown would actually feel good, as if she were getting the punishment she was due but could never sufficiently inflict upon herself.

I relate. I beat myself up, maybe with even more pain than rocks could inflict. Do you? I beat myself up for all I have done wrong. For things others have done wrong. For things I wish hadn't gone wrong. For things I will likely do wrong. Those words to my husband. Those punishments I gave my kids. That old friend I excommunicated. That lie of old I told. All of it. And more.

It is easy to feel like a target. It is easy to feel like God will bust you, rip you, show you a lesson, expose you, and then throw you into a den of hungry lions so that now you can *really* learn. It is easy to hear the words "You'll get what you deserve." This pain is real. It almost hurts your bones.

No wonder it's scary to bare it all. It's scary to get busted. No one likes the picture of conviction, the head shot where your hair is a mess and your face is downcast and zebra-striped with running mascara.

It is a horrible picture. No wonder we try to run and hide.

Does conviction taunt you? Do you feel it from days of old?

I imagine this was her. A woman probably so beautiful on the outside and yet so torn on the inside. I relate to that.

Heart beating out of her chest. Throat nearly choking on her own faults. Sin sitting heavy and damning in the air. Eyes shut, knowing her pain was about to become very real. Knowing the gavel of law would leave her bloody.

Did she hate herself?

She may have. I might have.

But Someone didn't.

One in the crowd.

One who saw.

One who knew.

One known to speak out on behalf of the voiceless.

Strong and kind, filled with truth and grace, the Lion and Lamb spoke, reigning above the heavy silence. "Let any one of you who is without sin be the first to throw a stone at her" (John 8:7).

He speaks the same words over us. Do we hear Him?

Sinners have no room to be haters. He lays it down, and the final verdict declares freedom: there is no room for us to be haters.

Haters of self. Haters of forgiven mistakes. Haters of those other ones with similar sins.

Have you left room for those things?

"The Spirit and the bride say, 'Come!' And let the one who hears say, 'Come!' Let the one who is thirsty come; and let the one who wishes take the free gift of the water of life" (Rev. 22:17). Come and get it! Walk on up! Take a drink.

The "water of life" is a free gift. It is what we don't deserve, but we get it all the same, and when we open it, we say, "Wow, You love me this much? Forget sin—I want you!" (see John 8:11). Ever noticed how much a gift can bring healing? This one certainly does.

It is ours to see. It is ours to run over to and pick up. It is ours to open.

It is here that courage talks. Both Lion and Lamb arise. Lion proclaims ferocious ownership of all things *you*, for His den will be your eternal home. Lamb speaks tenderness, kindness, and healing deep into your wounds. The Spirit confirms all of this and does much, much more.

The Spirit *seals* us, engraving or impressing on us all things Christ. He does this without fail until the day of eternity, a day that is guaranteed (2 Cor. 1:22). He *confirms* to our very soul that we will be with God forever. He *pleads* for our deepest needs through groans that we can't muster on our own (Rom. 8:26). He *fights* and *prays* on our behalf. He *reveals* the very mind of Christ to our minds that are so often focused on this world (Rom. 9:1; 1 Cor. 2:10). We, in turn, hear verdicts and pleadings afresh. We become aware of how Christ advocates for us and defends us (1 John 2:1). We feel wrapped up and contained in Jesus until the day of our glorious becoming (1 Cor. 13:12).

All of this is working in us as we are abiding and being with God. This is wild stuff. Spirit stuff. And it is so impactful and meaningful and pressure-less that you might just need to go back and read that previous paragraph again so it can sink in. So it can work its way into your actual day.

Let this truth mean something to you. Let it form a new belief and push out an old lie. There is so much that God is doing, without even an ounce of you involved—that is how much He loves you.

This truth assures me. It assures me that we can't go under when the mind of Christ, the Spirit, rules over us. Sure, we might hear that old song play, "We will, we will rock you." But then we can remember that Jesus never throws stones. He lays them down so His arms can embrace us in love.

It is this thought that can move you from being a pauper girl to a prized possession. It's this thought that makes me feel like I am a chosen one. It is this thought that makes me feel like I am part of *more*, a movement of love—His church—His bride. Glorious. Resplendent. Beautiful. Walking, working, and changing the world.

Holding each other until Jesus comes again.

Wearing white instead of the old clothes of our scandalous past.

Robed in riches, not torn up ruins and rags of wrong.

Standing in the splendor of true love, not bowing under the pressure of demanded love.

This makes me feel wanted.

Kept well.

Sure, war rages, but we are protected, supplied, and soon to be rewarded. For us, the water of life is free and ready for our consumption. Bullets may abound, but they ricochet straight back to hell, where they came from.

And yes, all this stuff, this bad stuff is around; yes, it happens, but so did Jesus and He will happen forever. Let this truth calm you. And then, when you hit those calamities, let it touch you again. Write it as a little note for yourself, stick it in your back pocket, and pull it out whenever you need to be reminded. Jesus rules; His throne is above it all. Eventually it will sink in as a new belief.

Eventually you will believe it so much you will be able to stand. You will stand because your righteous and pure Lord stands above all the wreckage, all agendas, and every fray. You look in the mirror and see Him—the one thing in this world you can rely on.

And for that, right in the center of the carnage and surrounded by mean ones, you will cheer, "You are victorious!" And He smiles.

Anxiety flees.

And what you will know more than anything else is that you are His and He is yours. Your steps get light and your breathing gets fluid because you know that wherever you are going with Him, the real destination is joy. So you grab hold and get ready—for it is bound to be "something else"!

Only He knows where you are going, and you are learning to trust Him more each day. And you feel pretty much okay with this idea.

This is an improvement from where you once were, for you realize that the stink, the decay, the old, the ugly—*the past*—doesn't have to define you. So you step back a bit, brace yourself, nod at it, yell at it, shed a tear, stomp your feet, throw a fit, and hate on it. And when you're done, you grab His hand. You know Love is with you. And what you see, before you try to push ahead, is His face. You see His love, love with no rocks, love that feels sadness over your past.

It means something. So you turn to Him and whisper, "Forgive me. I am sorry. You take this thing. Bury it. I can't carry it anymore."

And when you can, you really, truly let it go. You release, knowing that the Savior will save your story far better than you ever could. You breathe deep. You fill your lungs. You return to life. You realize you don't have to have it all figured out. You don't have to do the untangling. You don't have to make sense.

You exhale.

The Lord simply has to do the work. He simply has to speak. "The Sovereign LORD says to these bones: I will make breath enter you, and you will come to life" (Ezek. 37:5).

We come alive. What was fractured is healed.

## Something to Chew On

**A Greater Story**: God sees the details, the pain, the hopelessness, and the agony. He sees the ruins—ruins that often are easier left destroyed, because digging up the old makes you unsure if you'll ever reach the new.

But the small measure of hope is this: what others can't fathom, God already knows. What I can't stand is what Jesus fell for. What burden I can't carry, Christ has. He has won. He is winning. And He will win.

Will I trust that? Will I release my burden to Him? The past is yesterday and I live in today. The pain was yesterday and His healing is today.

So, less of me and more of Him. Less questioning and more trusting. Less of being a victim and more of being a victor. Because what I have is what I need: Emmanuel, my God who is with me, won't ever leave me. So I'll take what I can get—which is really the fullness of all I've ever needed. And, in this, I know I'll end up okay.

He has established my way. He's blessing it every day. He's creating it for His glory, weaving a greater story, not by my doing but through His reflection—a reflection of redone, reimaged, remade, recovered, restored, and reimagined. And I am rebounding, responding . . . solely by remembering Him.

With this remembering, I end up seeing things. Like Him not just carrying the cross but also me, that scared little girl—carrying me right into the cries of His heart, the healing of His blood, and His raw humiliation so that the reality we experience together, in regret, in sadness, and in anguish, swallows the heart-eating wounds of burden, baggage, and bile whole, through His love.

So even though it may be a moment-by-moment kind of fight, still, the Healer waits. Jesus waits. Ready and willing to rescue. Understanding my insides, so together, we may conquer.

# Afterword

## *Whatever Happened, It Counts*

If you think you're too small to have an impact, try going to
bed with a mosquito.

Anita Roddick, founder of The Body Shop

At this point, I want an earth-shattering bang of a send-off
for you. I truly do. I've imagined fireworks and rainbows
and waterfalls. I have even considered the word *grenade*, which is
probably taking things a tad too far. I have imagined tears and joy
and life and peace. I've thought about normal books, and how in
normal books this is where bows are neatly tied, where send-offs
have gusto, and where all the Is are dotted and Ts are crossed. I
so badly want to send you off this way.

Yet, stepping back, I can't help but think how sending people
off all Christmas-stylized, lit and tinseled, really has never done
Christ any justice and simply distracts true followers like you. So,
real is going to get more real here, friends, as I trust the Spirit to
do what He does best: bring the Word alive in His unique way in
your heart.

What I'm not going to tell you is:

1. You are now fearless. Go live wildly; you have beaten your every fear.
2. You have it all figured out—so live in peace, joy, and love in service to the Lord.
3. There is no fear in love, so stop fearing and start loving (aka, if you can't do this, there is something wrong with you).

No, I am not going to tell you these things, my friends. While some parts of them are true and some parts are not, sometimes it is the coming to terms with our own truth that actually sets us free. I don't know your timeline, but I do know that God wants to handle these two words (ahem: *set free*) one-on-one, hand-in-hand, and in conscious partnership with you. He reserves the right to decide when "set free" is achieved.

And perhaps you have been freed. Perhaps you partially are. Perhaps you've had epiphanies. Perhaps you have a new sense of yourself. Perhaps you are becoming aware of God's presence. Perhaps you are more aware of your own.

Perhaps you are making progress. Perhaps you hate yourself a little less. Perhaps you are seeing a greater cause emerge. Perhaps you are living encouraged. Perhaps you feel known. Perhaps you are being comforted.

All places are equally valuable, because this is where God wants you to be. All hats off to God for His work! All applause for His perfect timing. A standing ovation for what He is about to perfect in you.

He is faithful and will be faithful.

But let me tell you that you don't have to have it all. I refuse to pigeonhole progress into something we can call "finished." The finish line is called *heaven*, where we will all be perfected. While sometimes in life we take strides and find instant freedom, healing, or deliverance, other times we pant, huff, and puff all the way over to victory. God knows this, and He doesn't condemn us for it. He doesn't hand out demerits based on performance. He doesn't hate on us because we don't put on our big-girl panties and get ourselves together. He doesn't, and I won't.

I am tired of the demands. I am ready to just *be*. Be me. Be free. Be who He has called me to be. No pressure. No burdens. Just coming to Him and living in peace. Aren't you ready?

One thing I do know, dear child of God, is that God's heart beats for you and for me, for us hurt ones, arm-crossed ones, seemingly sad ones, pensive ones, unsure ones, trepidation-filled ones—even the three-feet-shorter versions of us. Relentlessly He chases us. Big and small, grown and still immature, learning and growing—He is Alpha and Omega, He was and is and is to come (Rev. 1:8), and He's in all places. He is healing the fear-filled gals we were yesterday and the growing-courageous gals of today.

He always wants to speak. I think His tailor-made message today, for our heart, might sound something like this.

*Dear child,*

*When I see you, I adore you. I delight in you. I am proud of you. You have come so far. But I have small things to remind you of, dear one, as you walk like a pilgrim without a home, a voyager not knowing your destination, and a pioneer of a hated cause. Have no doubt, small one, following Me is not easy. It requires courage, for you will head straight into the wars of this world and will be hit by intense insurrection. Expect that.*

*But before you abort your mission, please take note of those I call My children. The non-know-it-alls, the reliant ones, the listening ears, the hopeful voices, the I-don't-have-it-all-together few, the just-do-it kinds. I call the weak, wounded, and war-torn. I call the rising, the surviving, and the becoming—this means I call you.*

*In order for you to walk in boldness, you must know a few things. Take them, hold them, draw on them, rely on them, lock them up, and place them over your heart like a locket sealed by the Spirit forever and ever more. For these things will forge steadfastness, endurance, and perseverance within you—they will carry you all the way to where you need to be: home, forever and ever in safety, sanity, and complete health.*

*I want this for you, but until then I want to remind you:*

*This is not your home; don't you dare let appearances fool you.*

*I don't mark victory with a finish line, and I don't care how long your laps take as long as I am with you.*

*I don't expect a perfect performance; I love to uplift my fallen ones along the way.*

*I know that you're becoming, and that doesn't make you unbecoming.*

*When discouragement pants with his bad breath, my Word will bring you fresh air.*

*Your distance traveled is just far enough to guide others down that same path.*

*I have shared My light so you can spread it far and wide.*

*It's not about big missions but hearing My small voice—and obeying it.*

*It's not about loud applause but the small voice that claims a tiny victory against fear.*

*Others don't determine how well you are tracking; Jesus already declared you well.*

*Your identity is not a reflection of others' opinions but of Me.*

*Your ability to step back provides Me the ability to step in.*

*Temptation will knock, but that doesn't mean you have to answer the door.*

*My voice doesn't chastise you, and neither should yours.*

*Prayer will always carry you through when you don't know what to do.*

*When you die to yourself, you become alive to Me.*

*My home will always be your home—and there is no other place like home.*

*I have set a table for you. I have prepared a room for you. I wait for you.*

*I can't wait to throw open the gates to embrace you with the undammed fullness of My love.*

*Dear child, there is something else you should know: you have gifts. You may not even realize it, but they are powerful. I have entrusted them to you as a present delivered by the Spirit to lead, to bless, and to point others to Christ. They look like love, joy, peace, forbearance, kindness, goodness, faithfulness, gentleness, and self-control (Gal. 5:22–23).*

*Wear them like a locket of My faithfulness. Open each one carefully and look at it as something not achieved by your merit but handed out because of My great love. Don't be afraid to ask for more. I want to give you My best.*

*I grow your fruit and make it abundant and plentiful so that you can bring your barrels of delicious goodness everywhere—to all, to the homeless, hungry, and freezing folk. You see, when they taste and see that the Lord is good, they will want more—and that is the point. Suddenly, seeds from My fruit get planted and then the harvest is plentiful. I want this. The nourishment is satisfying, the colors are vibrant, the people are well. I become well and alive in your land. This is My cause—and you're more than a part of it; you are the bearer of Me.*

*Don't fear your light. Take the risk to be more than a flicker; be a bonfire that lures the world in to wonder what I will do next. Expand. Become contagious. Don't fear your light but fan it. Don't run from your pain but step into it. Carry your shield of faith, wield your Sword of the Spirit, and follow the light of Christ that outshines any darkness. You'll see where to go and you will make it there, even when blood and rage and terrorism and opponents and sour relationships and ugly opinions and threats and suffering and death hang nearby. Just follow that light—all the way home. All roads lead there for you, My believer.*

*Keep walking—that is all there is to it.*

*No pressure, child. I will grow you; just abide in Me, stay attached to My vine, and buds will happen. And don't you dare forget these words: I do not despise small beginnings. I rejoice to see the work begin (Zech. 4:10). Your mission is just to bring My small calls to fruition.*

*One final thing, a thing I would be remiss not to say: daughter, I know this world doesn't always feel like a safe playground, and it actually looks much more like wild territory. Risky territory. Raw territory. Salivating, rabid-wolf-prancing territory. Hunt-or-be-hunted territory, where the world seems to be on the verge of self-imploding at any moment.*

*Know this: I know all of that. I see all of that. I am in control of all of that. I don't love all of that madness, but I always handle the resulting sadness.*

*So, child, rather than chiding yourself for "getting extra extreme again" or Googling "Am I a hypochondriac?" or studying terrorist tactics or embracing survivalist modes or thinking out the best escape routes, how about just being? Just being with Me?*

*I long for you to enjoy My presence that is snuggled deeply at home within you. If you feel Me in you and My Words reside in you, you will be much more aware that I am protecting you. It's not Google you need, it is Me. That is it.*

*You and Me.*
*So don't be afraid to tell Me:*

*I am scared.*

*I am really scared.*

*I am scared of the idea of really losing all of myself to*
*You.*

*I am scared that I will shine too brightly to ever be liked.*

*I am scared of what You might have me do.*

*I am scared for the church because I don't know if at all*
*times, in every way, we will stand strong.*

*I am scared for my brothers and sisters who are facing*
*incalculable pain and agony.*

*I am scared for myself because I don't know what I will*
*do when harder, painful times hit.*

*I am scared at the thought that when push comes to shove,*
*I am not sure if my words will stand for or defame*
*my Savior.*

*Saying or thinking these things does not mean you have*
*lost all the marbles gained in this book and are now back*
*at ground zero. It means you are moving toward the word*
*fearless.*

*This word much more means "to fear less." This word*
*means to get just a tad more bold, an inkling more coura-*
*geous, an ounce more vulnerable, and a grain more willing.*
*Becoming fearless is done step-by-step. It is what I cheer,*
*because only I know how far each step will take you. Only I*
*am aware of how one day you will look back and say, "Wow,*
*we did that, God? Look how far we came."*

*I cheer this kind of stuff. When you let My love move in*
*to help you actually fear less, that's when the heavens nearly*
*shake the earth with their victory dance on your behalf. Your*

*future home, rising up on account of you, swirls in the glow of ray-filled skies and promises you a glorious existence that goes far beyond your so-called paltry one.*

*Oh, there is so much more I could say. It boils down to this: I delight in you. Choose to remember that.*

*So until we meet face-to-face in the comfort of your forever home, just walk by the Spirit and choose to really believe, as you repeat to yourself again and again like a lost girl in a far-off land: "There is no place like home. There is no place like home. There is no place like home."*

*For home waits in eager anticipation of your arrival to robe you as fully safe, recovered, and restored. Not just for a moment or for a century, but* forever. *Until then, fear less.*

> *Love, your affectionate*
> *and waiting Daddy,*
> *Father God*

## Living His Heartbeat

Friends, I have something else to tell you before you shut this book: to continue my fear battle, I need you.

I really do.

I need to hear your battle cries, your wounds, and your sky-lift stories. I need to hear your truth. I need to hear your epiphanies. I need to relate to your heart.

I feel desperate to hear of God's continual faithfulness.

I don't know, but maybe, just maybe, you also need to hear mine. We need to hear something that says to us both, here, in this place, in the small confines of our boxed-in life, that we can be okay together. We can be whole, we can be one of our own kind—the club we never really wanted to join but still one where we are entirely "in," where we "get each other." One where real knows real. One where honest breeds honest. One where open means opened to light. For then our secret handshake will ultimately point to God, in a way where others see He is pointing right back at us. Do you know what I mean?

I think we sisters need to band together.

Because, frankly, I am so tired of pulling apart. Aren't you? I'm tired of battling, of warring, of stroller judgments. I'm tired of politicking, of social media banter, of sizing up nails. I'm tired of insecurity, of vacation comparing, of striving, of rapid-fire opinions—and I'm even tired of debating theology. Time is too precious, my dear girlfriends (I hope I can call you that by now).

God is showing me that if we fear each other we have only handed a wedge to the devil and invited him to place it between us. *Welcome, confuser and abuser! Do what you do best—split, divide, and keep us in our square boxes of hurt, judged and beaten by the world.*

Time is too critical, our land is too polarized, the devil is too prevalent, and our heart is too much in need of Jesus's love for this. God doesn't care about our social measuring; He cares about our heart, our small gift of anything that is poured out at His feet. For then we pull up a chair in the center of the Spirit's home, we sit down, we breathe in, and then we exhale His love—and this is what it is all about, for when a fragrance like that is outpoured, the world longs to inhale it.

It blots out the rot of yesterday, it pushes aside self-reproach, it overpowers jealousy, it combats fear, it quells anxiety, it beats down threats, it puts things into the perspective of eternity, and it deepens relaxation.

When you enter into God's heart and sit down in the presence of His Spirit, suddenly your heart becomes baby-skin soft, tender, and sensitive. Like this: "I will give you a new heart and put a new spirit in you; I will remove from you your heart of stone and give you a heart of flesh" (Ezek. 36:26).

This is the tribal call for you. Can you hear it? It is God's love singing out for us. For me it sounds like learning, like welcome, like hope and life and peace. It sounds something like: *Come. Sit in My heart and let My Spirit rouse you. Then rise, My child—rise, dance, move, chant, dig your toes in deep; find who I made you to be and then share My love, commissioned. Go ahead: be unafraid and light a great mission.*

And remember: the God who is in you can never leave you.

# Join Us

I can't stand to think this adventure will end here, because it won't—it can't. I can't stand to think of leaving you, for we have come so, so far. I can't stand the thought of not knowing your personal voyage. In fact, I won't have it.

Because God has truly put transformation on my heart for each of you, I want to offer you something that I believe will help you progress even further on your fear-fighting journey. I have created an "Uncover Your Calling" quiz. Now that you ushered some of that fear out the door, it is time to make room for greater purpose! That is just what this quiz will do; it will help walk you up to the unique calling God designed you for. Because the truth is, you can only walk in your calling when you know what it is. This quiz is a tangible way to learn more about yourself and to identify your next steps.

Visit www.fearfightingbook.com to take this quiz and to start moving ahead in it. You will also find inspirational videos, tools, tips, and connection with others. You can submit your own story and read other people's stories. I encourage you to also join my Facebook page (Kelly Balarie—Author & Speaker), where you can take part in the "4 Weeks to Fearless Challenge" and connect with others who want to press in to greater courage.

I want to hear from you. If you are fighting fear in your day, tweet about it. Let me know at @kellybalarie, using #FearFightingBook, and share a fear or a tip that helped you win over fear. You can share it on Facebook too! Either way, just let me know how you won in faith. I can't wait to hear from you. Keep me updated on your progress!

My goal is that through it all we share, we virtually hug, and we love. We can't allow our progress to end here. Right now is the time to grab hands, sisters in courage. God has greatness in store for each of us. I want to see it play out.

The world waits. The time is now. We are the change-makers. With all this, we have to remember the Spirit won't let us down, either—after all, He is life and peace (Rom. 8:6).

# Group Study

## A Twelve-Week Fear-Fighting Challenge

**Week 1:** *Read Chapter 1*

### Stick This in Your Pocket & Hold on to It

If you walk out into the unsafe, you nearly can't help but find yourself safe in God's arms. What could be better than that?

Destination bravery means you step where you can't see. But as you step, an *Alice in Wonderland*–like stepping stone wonderfully appears. You get where you were supposed to go, even though you had no sane idea of where you were supposed to go to begin with. And in the end, you make it.

### Lighting the Match

"The Spirit of the LORD will rest on him—the Spirit of wisdom and of understanding, the Spirit of counsel and of might, the Spirit of the knowledge and fear of the LORD" (Isa. 11:2).

Close your eyes and invite the Spirit to:

1. Lead you in all wisdom and understanding.
2. Awaken your heart to the Word of God.
3. Pour out His counsel, might, and knowledge.

Listen—do you hear anything? What do you feel? Do you believe God wants your ears to hear with greater sharpness?

_____

_____

_____

**Fanning the Flame**

Jesus leads the way into fearlessness. His words walk us from unsteady to steady simply by the grasp of His outstretched hand.

Read Matthew 14:22–33. What does this story personally say to you about fear? Look for a fresh word.

_____

_____

_____

### A Shine-Bright Assessment

"Wake up, sleeper, rise from the dead, and Christ will shine on you" (Eph. 5:14).

Arise! Let the eyes of your heart open! Wake up your sleepwalking being. Break out of the shell that has kept you trapped in the defensive covering of nothingness. Break through to light. You are seeing things afresh. "Everything exposed by the light becomes visible—and everything that is illuminated becomes a light" (v. 13). The Spirit lets you see it so you can be it.

So arise from the dark, get up, stand tall; Christ in you, the hope of glory, is the answer to a waiting world. He has brought you from a hump of ashes to a million little sunrises, from dry bones to Spirit-guided motion, from hatred to love. Let the cry of your heart release to scream, "Hallelujah, Hallelujah, Hallelujah!" and see His glory ripple into the world's coffins, the antagonists' mindsets, and barren soil as His hand resets the unrest and unbinds the bound.

"Arise, shine, for your light has come, and the glory of the LORD rises upon you. See, darkness covers the earth and thick darkness is over the peoples, but the LORD rises upon you and his glory appears over you" (Isa. 60:1–2). When you read this, can you believe these words for yourself? What do you hear that holds you back from believing that God might do something magnificent for you?

### Fear-Busting

#### *Five Practical Tips to Find an Ounce More Calm*

1. *Fear.* Go ahead and do the deed; let your fear flow. Then magnify it twenty times. If you think you left the oven on, imagine your whole house burning to the ground. How would you and God go about handling it together? How bad would it be? Could you do it?

2. *See worry for what it is.* Close your eyes. Imagine you are carrying a ball and chain for each one of your worries. Feel yourself holding a ball for each problem. Label each ball with your worry. See it for what it is—and that is it. Don't get angry at yourself, don't berate yourself, don't hate yourself, just label it. Now walk it up to the foot of the cross, open your arms, and let the weight fall. Ask Jesus, "Can you hold this for me?" Let it go.

3. *Read a Bible verse before bed*. Repeat it in your mind again and again. See yourself adopting it, putting it into action, living it, learning it, holding it, and whatever else you can think of. Keep returning your mind to that verse.

4. *Find thanks*. Write down ten things you are thankful for. Dwell on thanking God for these gifts throughout your day.

5. *Remember what the Lord has brought you through*. Remember the trials, the tribulations, and the injuries you have endured. Remind yourself how God has never dropped you nor forsaken you.

Commit to doing one of the above, and share your progress with your group.

### More to Think About

Write down your greatest hope, dream, and vision.

_____

_____

_____

What fears have held you back from accomplishing it? Why?

_____

_____

_____

What risk might there be in taking a small step toward it by faith?

_____

_____

_____

## Week 2: *Read Chapter 2*

### Stick This in Your Pocket & Hold on to It

Fear fighters emerge when they stop ducking and start diving, with God, into the exact fear that wants to take them down. The more they press in, the more God presses out.

There is probably nearly nothing God wants to do more than take the barrier blocking bold and kick it back to hell where it belongs.

### Lighting the Match

Love overcomes fear.

- How do you want others to love you when you are hurt?
- Do you love others in this way?
- What fire are you venturing through right now?
- How might God be using that fire to bring you to holy ground?

### Fanning the Flame

What does it mean to fear God? How might you apply this to your daily life? Read the following Scriptures:

- Proverbs 1:7
- Proverbs 8:13
- Proverbs 14:27
- Luke 1:50
- Deuteronomy 10:12

How might the idea of fearing God actually work to reduce your daily fears?

How has Deborah inspired you to be fiery? What would you have to leave behind? What would you have to put on?

Checking in: How did you do with your "Practical Tips to Find an Ounce More Calm" from last week? How did you find them making a difference in your life?

**Fear-Busting**

**Awakening Courage:** If living as a modern-day fiery woman means following the fiery women in this chapter, which step could most change your life if you adopted it?

How might you put that into action in your life?

## More to Think About

Did you know that when firefighters approach a fire the first thing they do is find the source of the fire and any likely risks associated with that source? The predominant fire is not God's allowance of trials but rather the negative reaction of our heart. What is the source of the fire in your heart that you may need to put out?

Become aware of your fears:

- Pray and ask God to reveal your fears.
- Use a journal to mark the times where you felt abandoned, rejected, unsafe, or unloved.
- Discern the feeling you had in that moment.
- Continue this process every day as you go through this book. Take notice of what happens as you go through it.

Believe in the power of the Spirit and His ability to set your heart free as you journey through this book. Ask for courage, strength, and perseverance as you exhale your fears and inhale God's being.

### Week 3: *Read Chapter 3*

## Stick This in Your Pocket & Hold on to It

How do we stop fearing what we can't stop fearing so that we can actually do what God wants us to do? This is not a trick question.

*My ways + my thoughts = frustration, irritation, and the consequences of sin*

*God's new ways + my surrendered heart = a courageous, bold, Spirit-led life*

**Lighting the Match**

Who do you wish you were? What kind of person would you look like? Write it out.

_____

_____

_____

**Fanning the Flame**

What does it mean to flush out the flesh and flush in Super Spirit? What do these verses teach you?

- Romans 7:18
- John 3:6–8
- 2 Corinthians 5:16–18
- 1 John 4:2
- Ezekiel 36:2–27

In what areas of your life do you not feel super? In what ways might God want to show you that He is super?

_____

_____

_____

**Fear-Busting**

**Spirit Awakening:** The Spirit is . . .

- The Spirit of truth (John 16:13)
- The Word of the Lord (2 Cor. 3:17)

- Rivers of living water (John 7:38)
- Wisdom and understanding (Isa. 11:2)
- The interpreter of God's love language (1 Cor. 2:12)
- Our Comforter (Acts 9:31)
- Our Helper (John 14:16)
- Our Counselor (1 John 2:1)
- Our Advocate (John 16:7)
- The Spirit of the Lord (2 Chron. 20:14)
- The Spirit of God (2 Chron. 15:1)
- The Spirit of Christ (Rom. 8:9)
- The hand of the Lord (2 Kings 3:15)
- The visitor to all our thoughts (1 Cor. 2:11)
- The mind reader of God's thoughts (1 Cor. 2:11)
- The mind of Christ (1 Cor. 2:16)
- The equipper and the enhancer of truth (Exod. 35:31–32)
- Our artistic inspiration (Exod. 35:31–32)
- The discoverer of our value in God's kingdom (Exod. 35:31–32)
- The One who makes plain God's truth (1 Cor. 2:14)
- Our search engine of God's heart, who reveals the truth of our greatest searches (1 Cor. 2:10)
- Our life-giver (2 Cor. 3:6)
- The assigner of our calling (Acts 13:2)
- The revealer of deep and hidden things (1 Cor. 2:9–12)
- The unveiler of the extravagant callings for our lives (1 Cor. 2:9–10)
- The power who reveals Christ to our heart (Eph. 3:16–17)
- The One who convicts of sins (John 16:8)
- Our joy-bringer (1 Thess. 1:6)
- The One who brings freedom (2 Cor. 3:17)

What element of the Spirit most touches your heart? What names for the Spirit resonate most with you? Why? How might these words call you to fear less and to make progress?

**More to Think About**

Find Super God!

What promise of God particularly delights you?

_____

_____

_____

How do you notice God show up through your day?

_____

_____

_____

How might you expand the boundaries of your sight to see Him more?

_____

_____

_____

Have you noticed His beauty in the heart or actions of another? How?

_____

_____

_____

Ask God for the ability to see more of His love. Seek His love throughout your day. Wait with expectancy for His arrival. Thank Him for doing so. Start to delight in the God of presence.

## Week 4: *Read Chapter 4*

### Stick This in Your Pocket & Hold on to It

**How to tell if you have been targeted:** If you spend your life circling guilt and shame, you can be quite sure the devil is controlling much of your game.

If the devil can't completely devastate us from the outside-in, he'll work to decimate us from the inside-out.

When you know where and to whom you belong, you don't let the voice of a stranger lead you astray.

### Lighting the Match

Weapons are failing. Invasions are ineffective. Walls are dropping. What you see is that even while you are silent, your great and mighty warrior God is fighting for you (Exod. 14:14). He is working out all that you need. Even more, you see yourself on a horse, a warrior, a Deborah in the midst of attack, turmoil, and turbulence. Normally your hands would clench tight and your eyes would look for where to flee out of sight, but the One with you gives you a new radiance and a rock-hard surety in His cause. You aren't in a wilderness with no escape but on a great adventure with the One who provides all escape. You aren't ready to be ripped by savage beasts but caught up in the beauty of the Creator's creation. Innocence is being restored. Purity renewed. Wholeness replenished. Bounty is on the left and on the right.

Green pastures illuminate rest. Suddenly you realize this was never a battleground to begin with—it was always a garden. Sure, it has fallen people and mean villains, but what it mostly has is God. And, with the Spirit's power to set you free, there is no need for covering or hiding, because not an ounce of love is lost for a soul that sits in His presence.

**Fanning the Flame**

"If you then, though you are evil, know how to give good gifts to your children, how much more will your Father in heaven give the Holy Spirit to those who ask him!" (Luke 11:13).

How might truly believing you are a daughter versus being a runaway, an uncared-for and orphaned child, change how you receive the devil's crafty lies? Pray for the Spirit to guide you in your answer.

Attack back. What is the central wilderness lie that has attacked you from early childhood until present day? Write it here. I am:

Now, counter this lie with truth. God is:

What Bible verse is set to release you into the fullness of God's garden (repeat this day in and day out, aloud, when needed)?

_____

_____

_____

What D-word from the chapter (doubt, discouragement, despair, or devastation) chases you around? How can you see it approaching before it is too late?

_____

_____

_____

## Fear-Busting

> May you know not how strong the devil is
> but how strong the Spirit is within you,
> for then you will go to lengths
> you never dreamed you had in you,
> healing, loving, helping, guiding,
> seeking, finding, hoping, dreaming,
> giving, blessing, fighting,
> keeping an eye on eternity,
> a heart set on the Word,
> a life in surrender to the greatest keeper.
> May you make art
> by knowing God's heart.
> And shine bright
> as you put up a gallant fight.

You intended to harm me, but God intended it for good to accomplish what is now being done, the saving of many lives. (Gen. 50:20)

## More to Think About

Make a literal plan to put on the armor of God (Eph. 6:14–18). How can you do this day by day, moment by moment, in your life? (Example: When a fear surfaces, I will take a time-out to pull away from life and to meditate on a truth from God's Word that fights against it.)

The belt of truth:

_____

_____

_____

The breastplate of righteousness:

_____

_____

_____

Feet fitted to walk the gospel of peace:

_____

_____

_____

The shield of faith, which extinguishes fears and fiery arrows:

_____

_____

_____

The helmet of salvation:

_____

_____

_____

The sword of the Spirit, which is the Word of God:

_____

_____

_____

Praying in the Spirit on all occasions with all kinds of prayers and requests:

_____

_____

_____

**Week 5:** *Read Chapter 5*

### Stick This in Your Pocket & Hold on to It

It is not our abilities that make us able but His capabilities that prove to us He is more than able.

We get wealthy when we realize all wealth of knowledge is by God and according to God.

> Where can I go from your Spirit?
>> Where can I flee from your presence?
> If I go up to the heavens, you are there;
>> if I make my bed in the depths, you are there.

If I rise on the wings of the dawn,
   if I settle on the far side of the sea,
even there your hand will guide me,
   your right hand will hold me fast. (Ps. 139:7–10)

## Lighting the Match

I completely lost control once. Sure, I have lived in generally out-of-control states before, and that slow dullness is just enough to nearly kill anyone after not too long. Yet this was a different kind of experience, measured on an entirely different scale—one that nearly broke from the force of my weight. I lost entire and full control of my body. It was an out-of-body experience in some ways, though not as in losing myself to some weird alien invasion or a drug-induced hallucination or anything like that. But it was a situation of complete physical destruction, one where it seemed I was being cut, paralyzed, and swallowed whole all at the same time. One where my days seemed to be closing in. One where I couldn't breathe or do anything but try to scream. Truly, I would have done nearly anything to escape it. I don't want to go into too much detail, because if I did you would shut the book and abandon me, which would only leave me with a whole 'nother chapter to write so that God could fully heal me from my resulting shame. So let's leave this story as lightly touched as possible so as to preserve both your stomach and your will to read.

However, what you may benefit from knowing are the three things I learned from this physical trial:

1. The only way to make it through when you have nothing left is to call on the name of Jesus. Take it down one hundred decibels and the prayer sounds somewhat like this: "HELP! Help me! Jesus! God! I can't do it! I need you! Just help me! Now!" The eternal Paramedic, Lifeguard, and Great Physician is always on duty.

2. Having a glimpse of hell sure makes a person certain they've made the right decision to know, love, and live with Jesus Christ as their Savior. I never want to return, that's for sure. If you don't know Him, let Him chart your own adventure by turning back to the prayer on page 36.

3. The end of utter pain, agony, and loss of control is just the beginning of the eternal party for all who believe. If the worst comes to pass and you don't survive, and you lose all you have, you will make it big in heaven. And that is worth something.

Did you know the word *trust* in Hebrew is *bittachon*, or "lean on"? Which of the three realities above might help you risk falling back into the loving arms of the One who always stands ready to catch you?

**Fanning the Flame**

Tamar didn't have the greatest good fortune with husbands. Her first, Er, was flat-out "wicked" in God's eyes and the Lord put him to death. The second, his brother Onan, jigged and jagged around his responsibility to father a baby with Tamar. He died too. Is it any wonder their father may have had reservations about marrying his third son off to Tamar? I might have concerns too!

What was Tamar to do? How could she deliver a baby when God wasn't handy in delivering her a husband? Read Genesis 38:12–19. How did Tamar take things into her own hands?

How did Judah want to punish her (Gen. 38:24)?

_____

_____

_____

How did God's sovereignty still come to the rescue to save a conspiring sinner (Gen. 38:25–30)?

_____

_____

_____

How might you need God to save you today? Do you believe He will?

_____

_____

_____

**Fear-Busting**

*Courage Building*

Am I doing life on empty, exhaling fumes around me?

Am I doing life dreaming of a savior but not the One who saved me?

Am I doing life expecting people to give me all You've already offered?

Am I doing life yelling at actions and missing Your quiet whispers?

Am I doing life angry with another when it's Your love that placates?

Am I doing life listening to the old tapes instead of Your song
of truth?

Am I doing life running through the motions but forgetting
You're in motion?

Am I doing life knowing Your Word but missing Your heart?

Am I doing life thinking You won't save me and believing that
You hate me?

Or am I doing life knowing You are in me and trusting You
can't leave me?

**More to Think About**

A small seed of hope can move the mountains of hardship before you. "Truly I tell you, if you have faith as small as a mustard
seed, you can say to this mountain, 'Move from here to there,' and
it will move. Nothing will be impossible for you" (Matt. 17:20).

**Week 6:** *Read Chapter 6*

**Stick This in Your Pocket & Hold on to It**

Instead of looking for false strength in the affections of others, remember you need the approval of only One. When you
see Christ Jesus is your backbone (Ps. 62:2), people no longer
need to be.

**The Giving Girl**

There once was a girl,
And this girl loved her Father,
And she'd skip and hold His hand, seeing goodness
everywhere,

And she'd rest her head on the shoulder of His love,
    knowing she was safe,
And to Him she would run every morning, hearing His
    words that compelled awe and wonder,
And here, her heart would jump for joy at the astounding
    and unreachable depths from which she came.
And she'd run to tell His story, screaming His goodness
    far and wide,
And people would stop to listen because her heart was so
    proud,
And because they knew her too and her old numbing
    tricks.
They couldn't believe that grace abounded to this dirty-
    rotten soul.
The girl loved her Daddy,
And her Daddy loved her.
They were happy.

But time flew by.

And the girl grew more "spiritually mature."
She started to want to do everything, be everything, and
    get recognized for everything by those around her.
She sought to be the great deliverer of God's "happy," the
    counselor of godliness, and the hope of glory for those
    with a broken story.
She followed every rule, regulation, and requirement in
    order to keep Him happy, proud and overjoyed at her
    actions, knowing she was secure in love if she was
    "good enough."
And the girl grew tired, bored, frustrated, anxious, ir-
    ritated, resentful, and weary at this authoritarian pun-
    isher who stood ready to knock her down.
And the girl grew tired, bored, frustrated, anxious, ir-
    ritated, resentful, and weary at the people who were
    using up all her energy.

And her God grew distant, far off, out of reach, dusty,
worthless, a one-percenter who couldn't relate, an ivory
tower–sitter looking down from the judgment seat.
And her heart grew cold.
And His longed to meet her again.

*Her: God, this isn't what I expected.*
*Him: Nor I, dear child.*
*Her: I am sorry.*
She returned to her first love.
*Him: I have been waiting for you.*

How are you like the giving girl?

How might God also be calling you closer? What would He
say to you?

## Lighting the Match

"Do not conform to the pattern of this world, but be transformed by the renewing of your mind. Then you will be able to test
and approve what God's will is—his good, pleasing and perfect
will" (Rom. 12:2).

What does not being conformed look like to you? How might
you apply this to your life?

## Fanning the Flame

Nearly no one understood her plight. Likely they judged, criti-
cized, and made fun of this woman based on appearances.

*She's engaged, not married! How can she be pregnant?*
*Sinner! What a blasphemy to God!*

While appearances seemed to mark Mary the mother of Jesus
as sinful, God marked her as holy, loved, and chosen.

"Mary . . . was found to be pregnant through the Holy Spirit" (Matt. 1:18).

What might God love about you that others might not?

_____

_____

_____

What do you hold back for fear that you won't please others?

_____

_____

_____

God is less concerned about how we appear to others and more concerned about how we appear to Him. Write 1 Samuel 16:7 here:

_____

_____

_____

What truth from this chapter might God want you to hold on to as you walk toward His great purpose for your life?

_____

_____

_____

The Spirit wants to bring new life to you, just as He did to Jesus. New life. New hope. Death to sin. Hope in glory. Peace in your heart. How might God be calling you to see the perceptions of others in a new way? What new nugget of identity gleaned from this chapter can you hold on to about yourself?

_____

_____

_____

Get past pleasing people, and you will somehow get to God.

## Fear-Busting

**The Science of People Pleasing:** Did you know we can't even go out to dinner without feeling responsible for the person next to us? Our every bite seems to call us pig or prude. Studies say we eat to please the one sitting across from us.[1] They eat more, we eat more. No wonder we always seem to be in a constant battle with our weight. Our need to feed (aka the need to please) only partially feeds our heart that is oh-so-hungry to be accepted, loved, and adored. And what do we get in return? Empty calories and a growing belly.

*No wonder I love my hidden stash of chocolate. I can finally eat in peace, savoring the one piece of goodness that requires no performance.*

What else do you give up in exchange for making others "feel good"? Do you hold back your ideas to seem less intimidating? Talk less about Jesus around those who don't know Him as much? Change your speech when you are around "those" people? Act less Christian so as to not be offensive?

## More to Think About

"I'm not trying to win the approval of people, but of God. If pleasing people were my goal, I would not be Christ's servant" (Gal. 1:10 NLT).

"Whatever you do, work at it with all your heart, as working for the Lord, not for human masters" (Col. 3:23).

"Fear of man will prove to be a snare, but whoever trusts in the LORD is kept safe" (Prov. 29:25).

"It is better to take refuge in the LORD than to trust in humans" (Ps. 118:8).

Make a decision—will you serve God or serve people? Put everything you do today through that filter. See how you feel.

What might God think toward you as you follow through with this, simply in the moments of today?

_____

_____

_____

## Week 7: *Read Chapter 7*

### Stick This in Your Pocket & Hold on to It

Worry makes you imagine a great fight while you sit around and do almost nothing to accomplish anything. Because, well, you know. You *know*. With worry, all you do is wrestle yourself—and get nowhere. It's a losing game right from the start.

### Lighting the Match

What aspect of the Spirit means the most to you—Empowerer, Leader, or Filler? Why?

_____

_____

---

---

What aspects of W.E.L.C.O.M.E. might be the most transformative to you? How can you practically work these aspects into your life?

---

---

---

**Fanning the Flame**

Ask the Spirit to light truth and liberation in your heart in a fresh way. Listen for His truth as you read these verses.

Matthew 6:25–34

Proverbs 3:5–6

Philippians 4:6–7

Luke 12:24–34

What did the Spirit spark in you?

---

---

---

Read Matthew 14:26–32. What do you think compelled Peter to step out of safe and into risky?

---

---

---

Where might God be calling you out in the same way?

_____

_____

_____

What caused Peter to start to sink? What worries might have plagued him? What could make you sink in the same fashion (specifics)?

_____

_____

_____

How might Peter have fought against this uncertainty to walk powerfully in confidence?

_____

_____

_____

How does Jesus respond to those who doubt and waver? Does He catch those who fall?

_____

_____

_____

What sort of miracle might you see if you believed? Think of how the disciples reacted. What should your response be?

_____

_____

## Fear-Busting

### Awakening Courage

It is beyond getting good gifts.

It is beyond making it through unscathed.

It is beyond undoing myself when I want to wrap up in a
ball and fade away.

It is beyond all this.

It is beyond feel-good promises.

It is beyond church donuts.

It is beyond the community it brings.

It is beyond a remembered verse.

It is beyond trying to be saintly amid sinners.

It is beyond all this.

It is beyond my failings.

It is beyond my dreams.

It is beyond my achievements.

It is beyond my intentions.

But it is all about Jesus.

His face.

His cross, who He is, and how He endured it.

His Word—a dialogue, a conversation, a willingness, full
of thankfulness and presence.

I always thought it was about my grand plans and life
purposes.

He says, *No, child, it is simply about Me. Right here, right
now. It is about Me.*

I always thought it was about becoming great—for Him.

He says, *No, dear one, in Me you are already great.*

I always thought it was about doing and being more, being
the best Christian I could be.

He says, *No, it is simply about My glory-packed Son.*
Do you see Him? Do you know Him? Do you walk with
     Him every moment?
Find Him and find life.
Stay with Him and stay full of life.
Uncover His radiance and you will radiate.
*Come, dear one, I am the beginning and the end of all you
     need.*
*Let's dwell—Me with you and you with Me.*
*Together. Going. Present. Working. Active. Breathing.*
*I consume holy.*
*The cleaner your temple, the greater My residence.*
*So, let's move to transformation—whether big or small,
     whether today or tomorrow, whether as you thought
     or not.*
*Until one day I look at you and say, "Well done, good and
     faithful servant!"* (Matt. 25:23).

Pray and ask the Spirit of the Lord, "What does it look like for me
to drift with Your movement rather than by the tides of my worries?" Note what you hear. Share your reflections with your group.

---

---

---

### More to Think About

Today, choose to live *present*.

Living present means stopping the rat race of your mind when
you feel it start to get pushy. It means fighting the endless chatter
that is ready to move at a lightning-fast pace.

It means finding a place of peace in the space of worry. Here
are three ways to do this:

1. Get real about the real place where you stand. Notice your breathing. Take a survey of the people moving around you. Feel their hands as you hold each other. Talk to your God who is with you in this very moment. Stay in this place.

2. Reserve your worry for a different appointment time. Worry is friends with hungry, tired, and emotional women. Sometimes pushing off worry to another time is a woman's best bet. Then we are more balanced to deal with the imbalance of heart palpitations that may send us to the emergency room. Suddenly we see things for what they are—heartburn.

3. Breathe deep. I inhale peace, lightness, and the grace of God's love and exhale stress, unknowns, and the lies of the devil. It works. Keep at it until what is keeping you up at night is put to bed.

Bonus: if you wake up in the middle of the night with endless voices popping off—say the ABCs of God's attributes. God is affectionate, benevolent, and so on. I always fall asleep before I make it to Z.

## Week 8: *Read Chapter 8*

### Stick This in Your Pocket & Hold on to It

God has given us His best. The question is—will we take it and really believe it is ours?

Our calling doesn't disappear as we see another's calling appear.

### Lighting the Match

Then the mother of Zebedee's sons came to Jesus with her sons and, kneeling down, asked a favor of him.

"What is it you want?" he asked.

She said, "Grant that one of these two sons of mine may sit at your right and the other at your left in your kingdom."

"You don't know what you are asking," Jesus said to them. "Can you drink the cup I am going to drink?"

"We can," they answered.

Jesus said to them, "You will indeed drink from my cup, but to sit at my right or left is not for me to grant. These places belong to those for whom they have been prepared by my Father." (Matt. 20:20–23)

Have you been taking the Father's seat in a way you shouldn't be? Taking control? Doing without praying? Speaking before listening? Reacting before considering?

Do you find you chase Shifting Shadows more than you follow your great Chief? If so, explain.

**Fanning the Flame**

Read Genesis 29:15–30.

What cause did Leah have to be jealous of Rachel (see Gen. 29:17 for clues)?

What cause did Rachel have to be jealous of Leah (see Gen. 30:1 for clues)?

_____

_____

_____

What did their comparison and competition create (see Gen. 30:8)?

_____

_____

_____

How would you define this relationship of sisterhood?

_____

_____

_____

How would you encourage either one of them to act differently? How might they do so?

_____

_____

_____

Whom do you need to rectify a relationship with? How might you do it?

_____

_____

_____

### Fear-Busting

**Awakening Courage:** *I am wrapping and covering you. Inside, I've implanted a letter that sets forth the very story of My glory. It's authorized, certified, and signed by Me, but I have entrusted it to you. Hold it, carry it, and love by it. Take part in the epic I am unfolding. You are the fireplace to My fire; you hold what is so hot it has the capacity to remold lives. Don't fear My heat, wanting to push out from it, but embrace it, share it, and propel it into the world. I promise, you will not be left burned; there is nothing I cannot handle.*

*My love protects. My blood covers. My plans endure. You are the DNA of My very DNA, the life that I love, the one I see. I shield you from top to bottom and all the way around. You are safe in Me and I am safe in you.*

*I'll let you take part in My story's epic unfolding.*

*It is sealed by Me, the Spirit, who protects every grain of its nature.*

*This letter testifies of your irrevocable membership to My great club, called My kingdom.*

*The mission that's contained within can't be rewritten, undone, or remade.*

*Because it is only unveiled to the DNA of My DNA, those I protect with My iron-clad promise of love, My steel-headed, reinforced shield of untouchable.*

*In you, dear and faithful one, it is concealed. And to you it is being revealed.*

*Remember this.*

*Don't miss it.*

*It is the seal accomplished through My outpouring on your behalf, marked with the blood of Christ, for you are in Me and I am in you, making us blood of blood, merging, colliding, and flowing as one.*

*No matter what you do, where you go, or whom you encounter, be certain we belong to each other.*

*We move as one.*

*We mission in unity.*

*We create in tandem.*

*We walk unobstructed to bring My kingdom come.*

*Please, My dear, blameless one, be confident of the One who is always for you, despite how things look, feel, seem, or play out.*

*Because My leading is like no one else's. I have a unique plan set out just for you, dear child; keep your eyes on it—and go!*

What does God awaken in your heart as you read this? How might this change your perception that you are going through life alone?

_____

_____

_____

## More to Think About

He didn't come in high and mighty.

He wasn't notable in our sense of the word.

Some might have called Him "not so good looking."

He was different and outspoken.

He didn't care about façades.

He didn't give a hoot about accumulating wealth.

He wasn't caught up in the social norms.

He didn't abide by the social correctness.

He didn't bow down to anyone but His Father.

How can you choose today to be like Christ?

Perhaps it looks like loving the one you are prone to critique, condemn, or compare yourself to. How can you do things differently? When you pour out love, God pours in great courage to go a new way.

Note in your daily journal your progress and the person whom you encouraged.

## Week 9: *Read Chapter 9*

### Stick This in Your Pocket & Hold on to It

You can't really work to earn something that Jesus already paid for. Jesus said, "It is finished" (John 19:30).

When we say thank you, we start believing and standing firm.

Turn around—and stay around places God can be found.

### Lighting the Match

Many times, the fear of what will happen next is actually the fear that you can't handle what will happen next.

But rather than fighting this view, why not just lay down and submit to it? Why not let it topple you and move on? Sound crazy? Why not say, "Jesus, I am bound to mess this up. I always do. I need You to rescue me."

When we let Christ rescue, He rescues. When we let Christ be powerful, He is powerful. When we let the Spirit lead, He leads.

Sound too simple? "The LORD protects those of childlike faith; I was facing death, and he saved me" (Ps. 116:6 NLT).

## Fanning the Flame

Lay down, breathe deep. Breathe in for four counts. Hold for four counts. Exhale for four counts. While you breathe, inhale God's deep love for you, feeling it touch every part of your being. Become aware of each place it is reaching—your toes, your feet, your legs, and so on. Then exhale grace. See it going out into the world as you calm your body.

> And I pray that you, being rooted and established in love, may have power, together with all the Lord's holy people, to grasp how wide and long and high and deep is the love of Christ, and to know this love that surpasses knowledge—that you may be filled to the measure of all the fullness of God. (Eph. 3:17–19)

What comes over you when you quiet your mind to love?

_____

_____

_____

What might you need to do to live a life rooted and established in love? How would this look, practically, on a daily basis?

_____

_____

_____

What are all the ways God has been showing His love for you lately? Write the top three.

_____

_____

_____

What might it mean to be "filled to the measure of all the fullness of God"? How might you experience this more and more?

_____

_____

_____

### Fear-Busting

**Speaking Courage:** Speak it. Speak it loud and proud, just like Jesus did in the garden when the devil whispered the lies of "You'd better do something."

> Talk back with faith and say:
>
> God is perfecting what needs perfecting.
> My wait is the door to God's great.
> The best yet is just about to come.
> Waiting ground is the forging ground of authentic faith.
> The ring of waiting is the place where great fighters are made.

God doesn't half deliver. He bakes all cakes to perfection before He takes them out to let us indulge. God is more concerned with who I am than how happy I am; I am learning to be okay with this. Sometimes the wait is not about me but much more about one individual who needs to know Christ.

What truth stands out most to you? What other truths about waiting could you add?

_____

_____

_____

## More to Think About

### *Experience God!*

See what you most fear . . .

1. Close your eyes.
2. Ask the Spirit to reveal His heart toward this situation.
3. See the situation. Notice how you feel toward it.
4. See Jesus in front of you. Let Him stand with you and look at your pain or fear.
5. Thank Him for all the ways He cares for it, for you, and for the future.
6. In the quietness of your heart, what words, Scripture, and truth come to mind? What might He say to you about this exact issue?
7. Write in your journal, turn on a praise song, or offer a prayer of gratitude to your Lord.

He says, "Be still, and know that I am God; I will be exalted among the nations, I will be exalted in the earth" (Ps. 46:10).

## Week 10: *Read Chapter 10*

## Stick This in Your Pocket & Hold on to It

Rejection becomes of no consequence when you stand in the presence of the One transforming you into His beautiful image (2 Cor. 3:18).

## Lighting the Match

Write a love letter from God to you.

_____

_____

_____

Write a love letter from you to God.

_____

_____

_____

_____

## Fanning the Flame

Read 1 Corinthians 9:24–25.

What do those who run the race receive? How might this encourage you?

_____

_____

_____

There are five types of crowns reserved for believers. Investigate.

Read 1 Peter 1:3–5. This is the crown of _____.
How does this speak to your security?

_____

_____

_____

Read 1 Thessalonians 2:19. This is the crown of _____.
Read Revelation 21:4. How will this be possible?

_____

_____

_____

Read 2 Timothy 4:8. This is the crown of _____. Who
are the people who receive it?

_____

_____

_____

Read 1 Peter 5:4. This is the crown of _____. Read Acts
7:55–56. How might it look to see glory?

_____

_____

_____

Read Romans 8:18. What did Paul look forward to?

_____

_____

_____

How might this have changed his view of persecution?

_____

_____

_____

Read Revelation 2:10. This is the crown of _____. Read James 1:12. Blessed is the one who _____. How could you remain this way? How does the idea that you will receive crowns in heaven impact your fear of rejection today?

_____

_____

_____

### Fear-Busting

#### *Awakening Courage*

Rejection is love blocked.

Rejection is when you try your best and still get shot down.

Rejection is living opportunity yet being called failure.

Rejection is meeting an advice-giver when you're trying to be a heart-bearer.

Rejection is silence when you expected encouragement.

Rejection is a no when you wanted yes.

Rejection is trying only to end up tripped by one you love.

Rejection is believing you disgust God.

Rejection is seeing how God didn't come through for you.

Rejection is thinking that no matter what you will do, you won't be enough.

And you think that maybe you just arrived at the point—because you fall to your knees, probably exactly where God wanted you to be all along. And you reach out, hands wide open, and in humility you grab God's acceptance, hold it, examine it, wonder, consider, and ask, "Could I?"

And what you come to is the gentle touch of truth that is only delivered by One named Consoler and Comforter. For here, you see *you*. Not you and the mean ones, not you and the hurters, not you and the injury—just you and Him. And His plan.

You start to see all the things you swatted away. Truths such as other people don't define you. Dreams belong to God. His victory is permanent, His rejection was worth it, and there is no wasteland of defeat awaiting you.

Now you know things like feeling far away means it's time to draw near. God's gift and His call are irrevocable. No weapon forged against you shall prosper. By His stripes you are healed. The war has already raged, been fought, and is finished—He has won.

And so you see with fresh clarity that the choice is so obvious: the author of your life can either be people or God.

What do you see rejection as? How might God author your life in a new way? What might He speak to you?

## More to Think About

Investigate yourself. Think of someone who rejected you.

What did that person do (for example: left me out of a group gathering)?

_____

_____

_____

How did they act (selfish, judgmental, and so forth)?

_____

_____

_____

_____

Have you ever acted the same way that you wrote about above?

_____

_____

_____

In those instances, what were some of the reasons you acted that way?

_____

_____

_____

Can you forgive the person (people) who rejected you? _____
How has this rejection caused you to fear, cause pain in others'
lives, or numb yourself?

_____

_____

_____

Ask God to forgive you. Does He forgive you?

_____

_____

_____

Receive God's always acceptance and believe it is now yours.

For I am convinced that neither death nor life, neither angels nor
demons, neither the present nor the future, nor any powers, neither
height nor depth, nor anything else in all creation, will be able to
separate us from the love of God that is in Christ Jesus our Lord.
(Rom. 8:38–39)

**Week 11:** *Read Chapter 11*

## Stick This in Your Pocket & Hold on to It

You know you are living in the past when you think the only way to escape your feelings is to kill them, numb them, or run from them.

You can't really go under when the mind of Christ, the Spirit, is ruling over you. Sure, you might hear that old song play, "We will, we will rock you." But then you remember that Jesus never condones stoning.

## Lighting the Match

"Therefore confess your sins to each other and pray for each other so that you may be healed. The prayer of a righteous person is powerful and effective" (James 5:16).

Forgiveness is the exchange point of resentment and remorse for renewal and regeneration.

## Fanning the Flame

Unforgiveness makes your mind a constant battleground of good vs. evil.

It clouds your view of God.

It hinders your perception of the world.

It sends you forth in judgment.

It is the great boomerang of suffering.

It is one of the greatest barriers to growth, purpose, and life.

### Releasing Char and Igniting Fire

#### *A Releasing Prayer Process by We Want More Ministries*

"And pray in the Spirit on all occasions with all kinds of prayers and requests" (Eph. 6:18). Ask the Spirit: *Whom do I need to forgive?* Let your mind roll over father, mother, sister, brother, and so forth. Listen.

List person here: _____

List person here: _____

Speak each name to God. One by one, ask Him what you need to forgive each person for. (Listen.) Write what comes to mind here or in a journal:

_____

_____

_____

_____

Speak Aloud:

> *God, I choose to forgive _____ for any way or all the times he/she/they _____. I hand to You all the hurt, anger, regret, bitterness, rejection, loneliness, judgment, and sadness. I take back anything they took from me. I give back anything I took from them. In the power of Jesus's name I break off any unhealthy relational ties to _____. I turn away from any ungodly agreement or connection I made that goes against Your ways, Lord. Forgive me for anything in my life that came as a result of this sin. And I ask You to fill me with Your truth. Lord, I hand _____ to You. I bless _____ in Jesus's name and thank You for them. What do You have for me in exchange?*

What did you see, sense, or feel after you prayed that prayer?

_____

_____

_____

> *Holy Spirit, is there anything else I need to forgive* _____
> *for?*

What did you see, sense, or feel after you prayed that prayer?

_____

_____

_____

Repeat this as many times as you need to forgive.

## Fear-Busting

Your biggest fear may be your springboard to unshakable courage.
Your uncertainty may maximize your capacity for faith.
Your past scars show God brought you through—and will again.
Your agony may be your chance to see how much Christ cares.
Your gentle, God-centered approach when you do wrong may
be a new internal peace song.

How might small mind-shifts of positivity stamp out deep paths
of negativity? Write out three ways that you can see one of your
fears differently. Explain what "faith is belief in the things unseen"
(see Heb. 11:1) means to you.

_____

_____

_____

## More to Think About

How might Jesus be calling you to come to Him? Will you?

At the end of each day, take a personal inventory. Forgive who you need to forgive (even for minor offenses). Make a habit of clearing out the bad to make room for God's good. The less that covers your vision, the more you can envision all things good and all things God.

## Week 12: *Read the Afterword*

### *Prayer to Reduce Stress (Speak Aloud)*

*From today on, God, I choose Christ's power first and foremost. I choose to look for good, own Your plan, glean lessons from trials, and listen to the Spirit's prompting. With you, God, I am on to new things, brave things, and unknown things. Thank You that I am courageous; I made it through this book after all. Even more, I thank You that there is no weighted standard for that word courageous; it is not something that I make, build, or force. It is not something I have to have a daredevil spirit to own, nor something I demand of myself that I improve, but rather it is something You rewire in me as I let Your current flow.*

*With you, Father, I choose to fear the world less and fear You more. This will be my charge. May I remember it. Help me also remember fearing less is a process—and You delight in small progress. Each miniscule gain is a leap from where I came. May I hold on to this tiny grain of reality like a heavy trophy of incomprehensible worth. May I discount no progress or current moment where I can find joy through the simple words "thank you." Whether it is my first or my hundredth trophy, may I remember it doesn't matter. Even if I have fallen backward, even if I lose all my marbles, even if I wake up feeling like I am in a coma of regret, it is never too late to get up and start again. It is never too late to know that You have a greater teaching, a fuller epiphany, and a wider love ready to extend to me. May I hold on to that. May I never doubt it. It counts. It matters.*

*You are always at work. I can trust You. You are doing something. Help me reach out to grab Your hand that is always extended to me, even when I am cowering, shivering, and perspiring in fear. Amen.*

## More to Think About

As you trust Him, God:

Is with you and will strengthen and uphold you (Isa. 41:10).

Will guard your heart and mind (Phil. 4:7).

Will leave you peace (John 14:27).

Will drive out fear (1 John 4:18).

Will console your heart (Ps. 94:19).

Will comfort you (Ps. 23:4).

Will uplift you (1 Pet. 5:6).

Will provide for you (Phil. 4:19).

Will hold you strongly (Ps. 27:1).

Will never leave you (Deut. 31:6).

Will help you in times of trouble (Ps. 46:1).

Is encamped around you (Ps. 34:7).

Will free you from all fears (Ps. 34:4).

Is exulting over you with joy (Zeph. 3:17).

Will keep you safe (Prov. 29:25).

If you believe that, how might you live your life and your calling differently? What might you go and do today that would be one step closer to fear-less?

_____

_____

_____

Perhaps doing one new thing, despite your fear, might be the start of the best days of your life. What could that one new thing be?

_____

_____

_____

How can you make a small goal to accomplish it by moving just one step closer? Keep going in your goal-making, step-by-step.

_____

_____

_____

### Will You Lay It All Down to Follow?

In Mark 10:17–27, the rich man couldn't part with his money. What fear is hard for you to part with? Jesus knows that fear. He sees how you hold on to it for dear life.

Perhaps He would speak to you like the rich young man . . . but in a slightly different way.

To the rich man, He said, "If you want to be perfect, go, sell your possessions and give to the poor, and you will have treasure in heaven. Then come, follow me" (see v. 21).

To you He might say: "If you want to be perfect, stop relying on this fear and do something new, show my love, or minister in a fresh way, and you will have treasure in heaven. Then come, follow me."

Will you lay it all down and follow Him, or will you turn the other way?

Will you come and follow Christ?

What might that look like?

Join us at www.fearfightingbook.com to take the "Uncover Your Calling" quiz to help identify what God has uniquely fashioned you to do and be!

# Acknowledgments

God—Alpha and Omega, beginning and end—there is no start or conception of any sentence without you. Your Spirit has been a Guide of continual inspiration, vision, and fullness. If this book is to go entirely unread by anyone, anywhere, it cannot be deemed a failure, for the change in my heart has been unexplainable. This book was a risk. I went into it completely unsure if You would change me, grow me, and help me, but, in so many ways, isn't that posture of faith just how You like it? You can work with that. And You did. For this, I say thank You for making me a fear-less woman, thank You for helping me come alive to myself, thank You that You give me the space not to have everything all figured out, and thank You for the gift of being—with You. For joy is only gifted in the present moment. And now I know that opening this little package is what will radically rebuild my relationships. Thank You. And thank You for bringing Your Word to life—more specifically for teaching me how to understand and receive grace. You led the charge here, and You charged straight in to uplift my fallen pillars of courage. The ruins are rising. The pieces are no longer puzzles. The parts are no longer left unsure.

Half of me wants to write nearly this whole acknowledgment to You and, in fact, I think I will. I will, even though the other half of me is worrying what others will think. But I guess I'll just shrug my shoulders, raise my hands up to the sky, and say, "Who cares? Who cares what they think! I am becoming fearless. I am pursuing Your gentle breeze." And then I'll spin fast; just You and just me, all-in, moving as one, untouchable!

I have never been all that special, God, but You love me as if I am. Thank You. You took my Red Sea, placed your mighty staff in the center of it, ripped it open, and let me take one little insecure step after another to write this sweet declaration of dependence. Thank You. You aligned meetings and people and places and fire and rejections and pain because You wanted me to know humility is brave, serving is courage, and loving is power. My imperfect is Your perfect avenue to bring me to my knees and to a place of out-of-breath seeking. You brought me close to Your beauty. Thank You.

Thank You, God, for speaking to my heart by the power of Your Spirit, great calling, great mission, and an overwhelming weight of responsibility. Don't ever let me forget it. Don't ever let me fall by the wayside, which I very well could do. Let my every breath be You, let my every thought be peace, let my every word be encouragement, let my every action be love, and let my very life be humility. Break through my hardened exterior to make me soft to selflessness and free of judgment. May the plagues of pride, jealousy, or comparison never deter me. I acknowledge that all good things in this book are from You—the bad parts are most certainly me. Remove those parts from the memories of readers. May You shine. May they remember You.

Thank You, Father, Son, and Holy Spirit—You did it!

Thank you to all my other cohorts in fear-fighting (in no weighted order): Emanuel, this book would not be in existence without you. Michael, you keep my heart growing and my face smiling. Madison, your kisses mean everything. Mom, you exemplify selflessness.

Dad, you teach all-out pursuit of God. Sistahs and brothahs Katie, Theresa, Garrett, Elinor, and Joe, your encouragement and questions meant everything. Amanda Luedeke, thank you that I didn't have to wrestle you to get a shot.

Thank you, Baker team! Rebekah Guzman, you believed big and I can't thank you enough. Mark Rice, Eileen Hanson, Brianna DeWitt, Abby Van Wormer, Lindsey Spoolstra, Hannah Brinks, and Heather Brewer, you gave your all to this book and my gratefulness cannot be written in words.

Christi McGuire, your 24/7 editing expertise and encouragement were unparalleled. Kristen Reynolds, you kept me sane; you know all you did. Jim and Deb and the Martin clan, you were the first family hearers of the book; your feedback made my heart jump. Cindy, Sunny, and everyone at the More house, the Spirit-work done at your residence awoke a raging warrior daughter. Brooklyn Tabernacle, God knows you loved me.

Desiree Taylor, Sheena Lofton-Higgins, and Diane Vredenburg, every inch of prayer made this inch-sized book work. Katie Reid, Abby McDonald, Christy Mobley, Angela Parlin, Angela Nazworth, and Karina Allen, you all were my flashlights when I went in the dark. #RaRalinkup, you taught me encouragement is the greatest antidote to comparison and jealousy; you love so well. Neena, Karin, and Rosie, you all are my lieutenants in war; you are my cohorts in the grand fight and my Spirit inspiration. Julie Parsons, your nurturing love kept my heart beating at a time when it could have stopped. Rachel Macy Stafford, God showed me how much He cares for His daughters through you.

Lady on the airplane, you reminded me to be me and not some manufactured version of an iconic woman. To the gal who rejected me, you gave me wisdom only found through Christ. Julie and Heather, you have helped me carry the little girl to the foot of the cross. Anna Tobben, your prayers brought this book into being. Sue Stuart, your celebration and well-keeping of me was

God-ordained. Dawn Anderson, out with the garden and in with a different kind of woman-warrior made my proposal come alive. Allen Arnold, your words were instrumental; they made me sing childlike songs to my Daddy—and He loved them. Nikki Carlson, you are a fighter. Ray and Linda Lockery, thank you for investing in this fear fight. Maria Peterson, you kept my kids straight while I came undone upstairs. Jamie, you brought clarity to the mess that is called my mind. You nipped and tucked and yes, your fingerprints abound. Chad Cannon, you instructed me. Rob Eager, you gave me a blessing.

To fear: I knew you as dear, but now I know God is near.

To the Author of Romans 11:29, thank You for securing me in both this mission and Your desired outcome of it: "for God's gifts and his call are irrevocable."

# Notes

## Chapter 2  Dodging Obstacles

1. Alexandra Ossola, "This Woman Sees 100 Times More Colors Than the Average Person," *Popular Science*, October 13, 2014, http://www.popsci.com /article/science/woman-sees-100-times -more-colors-average-person.

## Chapter 3  Discovering Super Spirit

1. R. Barry Ruback and Daniel Juleng, "Territorial Defense in Parking Lots: Retaliation against Waiting Drivers," *Journal of Applied Social Psychology* vol. 27, no. 9 (May 1997): 821–34.

2. Brad J. Bushman, "Effects of Warning and Information Labels on Consumption of Full-Fat, Reduced-Fat, and No-Fat Products," *Journal of Applied Psychology* vol. 83, no. 1 (Feb. 1998): 97–101, http://dx.doi .org/10.1037/0021-9010.83.1.97.

3. Richard Driscoll, Keith E. Davis, and Milton E. Lipetz, "Parental Interference and Romantic Love: The Romeo and Juliet Effect," *Journal of Personality and Social Psychology* vol. 24, no. 1 (Oct. 1972): 1–10, http://dx.doi .org/10.1037/h0033373.

4. Daniel M. Wegner and David J. Schneider, "The White Bear Story," *Psychological Inquiry* vol. 14, no. 3 (2003): 326–29.

## Chapter 7  Worry

1. L. Sternheim et al., "Understanding Catastrophic Worry in Eating Disorders: Process and Content Characteristics," *J Behav Ther Exp Psychiatry* vol. 43, no. 4 (2012): 1095–103, http://www.ncbi .nlm.nih.gov/pubmed/22721602.

## Chapter 9  Waiting While Trembling

1. Walter Mischel, Ebbe B. Ebbesen, and Antonette Raskoff Zeiss, "Cognitive and Attentional Mechanisms in Delay of Gratification," *Journal of Personality and Social Psychology* vol. 21, no. 2 (1973): 204–18.

## Week 6

1. Julie J. Exline et al., "People-Pleasing through Eating: Sociotropy Predicts Greater Eating in Response to Perceived Social Pressure," *Journal of Social and Clinical Psychology* vol. 31, no. 2 (2012): 169–93.

# About the Author

**Kelly Balarie** is a fear fighter on a mission to set hearts free to pulse with greater peace and passion. As a writer, her fear-squelching words have been seen on *Internet Café Devotions*, (in)courage .me, *God-Sized Dreams*, *Christian Woman* magazine, *Relevant* magazine, and *Today's Christian Woman*. As a national speaker at women's and church events, her approach has been called "moving," "exceptional," "captivating," and "transformational." Kelly and her husband find themselves often on the move. Currently they are packing up to head to some US city even they have yet to determine. But God knows, and regardless, they know they'll be arriving with two toddlers in tow. You can find out more about Kelly on her blog (www.purposefulfaith.com), on Facebook (Kelly Balarie—Author & Speaker), and on Twitter (@kellybalarie).

# Connect with Kelly!

For more information and online resources, visit

## FearFightingBook.com

and

## PurposefulFaith.com

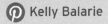 PurposefulFaith       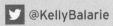 @KellyBalarie

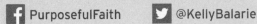 Kelly Balarie       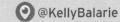 @KellyBalarie

# LIKE THIS BOOK?

## Consider sharing it with others!

- Share or mention the book on your social media platforms. Use the hashtag **#FearFightingBook**.

- Write a book review on your blog or on a retailer site.

- Pick up a copy for friends, family, or strangers— anyone who you think would enjoy and be challenged by its message.

- Share this message on Twitter or Facebook: **I loved #FearFightingBook by @KellyBalarie // FearFightingBook.com and PurposefulFaith.com @ReadBakerBooks**

- Recommend this book for your church, workplace, book club, or class.

- Follow Baker Books on social media and tell us what you like.

 Facebook.com/ReadBakerBooks

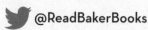 @ReadBakerBooks